Jude Weisenbeck, S.D.S.

THE LURE FOR FEELING

Landscape with bridge and willows by Ma Yüan of
Sung period
"I heard a thousand blended notes" . . . Wordsworth

Courtesy of Boston Museum of Fine Arts

THE LURE FOR FEELING

IN THE CREATIVE PROCESS

Mary A. Wyman

PHILOSOPHICAL LIBRARY

New York

To

my sister

EVA WYMAN DUNLAP

whose love of beauty

is

contagious

FOREWORD

Some years ago Chinese scholars were attempting to translate certain of their classics into English and were meeting great difficulty in finding words to use which would not mislead the English reader. Report has it that they solved their problem by using the English terminology of Whitehead's philosophy. Mary Wyman's study expresses such a connection.

Whitehead's *Science and the Modern World* first made everyone aware of the humanistic literary and poetic, as well as the mathematical and scientific, background of his thinking. Miss Wyman's studies reinforce this approach to his philosophy also.

Philosophers have recognized the aesthetic component of Whitehead's thinking. They also know the superficially dry and dull technical categories of his *Process and Reality*. Nowhere, however, to my knowledge, will the reader find the technical prose of Whitehead's great metaphysical work take on such aesthetically immediate concreteness as it does in the second chapter of the present book.

We are indebted to its author also for tying the romantic Goethe to the Romantic Movement of Whitehead's *Science and the Modern World* as we are grateful to her for establishing an essential connection between the whole artistic and mathematical sweep of Whitehead's philosophy and the greatest of America's poets.

Truly the author of this book has engaged in "adventures among books." Her readers now have the privilege of adventuring also.

F. S. C. NORTHROP
Sterling Professor of Philosophy and Law
Yale University

PREFACE

Adventures among books over an extended period have resulted in this collection of studies under the title of *The Lure for Feeling* in the Creative Process. The phrase, lure for feeling, as Whitehead uses it, suggests a mystical point of view, and a strain of mysticism is apparent in the major writers here considered. For himself, however, Whitehead would have rejected the name of mystic or idealist as unfitting. The evidence of the senses is too important to him, and the identity of man's bodily life with nature. Yet mystical insight both in poetry and philosophy often arises from perception through the senses. Such was the experience of Wordsworth, whom we link with Whitehead in recognizing beyond the ceaseless change of this world a transcendent lure for feeling, guiding all becoming to enduring value. The meaning of the lure as God in the world diffusing his power in his creatures is reflected also in Goethe and in Emerson, and seen most completely in Whitman. Even in John Burroughs there is an element of mysticism in his love of nature —an approach that he sees too in Emerson. That philosophy itself, like poetry, has a mystical character, Whitehead admits, for to him "mysticism is a direct insight into depths as yet unspoken."

This kind of insight into nature I have implied in a study of Chinese mysticism and Wordsworth; here Whitehead too is recognized as agreeing with Chu Hsi, the Neo-Confucian philosopher of the Sung period in Chinese history, in a mystical approach to the universe. It is the lure of *anima mundi* that is equally telling in the work of artists, poets, and sages in China, and in the voice of the greatest romantic poet in England. And it is a similar lure for feeling that plays so significant a part in Whitehead's philosophy of organism.

In my early teaching of romantic poetry following a sojourn in China, I had been impressed by a relationship between Chinese mysticism and the thinking of Wordsworth. Later study of Whitehead brought to my attention a resemblance to Wordsworth in their respective views of the creative process. I found also striking similarity between Whitehead's thought and that of Emerson and of Goethe, whose probable influence upon Emerson I had been pondering. All three had emphasized the continuance of nature's processes in human experience;[1] and all three had seen in the actuality of God in the world a power or lure, as Whitehead would have it, quickening animate life to possible attainment of value. The common ground of Goethe, Emerson, and Whitehead then was metaphysical—an area where poetry and philosophy meet. To show the convergence of their thought has been the aim of Chapter III, which has gradually evolved to become the heart of this volume.

As any approach to Whitehead involves a problem arising from his terminology, Chapter II has seemed necessary to clarify the terms used in his treatment of the lure for feeling and its function in the philosophy of organism. Because of the novelty in his meanings, a glossary has been added of those terms that seem most significant. It also appeared to me essential to indicate in Chapter II the possible hints that came from Plato in Whitehead's speculations on the lure and its function.[2]

In reading through the works of John Burroughs, I met again the ideas discussed in Chapter III, specifically as articulated by Goethe and by Emerson, whom Burroughs greatly admired. Not so certain as they of the actual presence of divinity in the world, he yet pondered with increasing intensity the mystery of all being, and recognized the metaphysical need of some immanent or transcendent power behind animate life. This need he saw more clearly through his intimate acquaintance as comrade and biographer with Walt Whitman. Like Wordsworth, Whitman was read with deep appreciation by Whitehead; and as Goethe at the beginning of his career called Spinoza his master, Whitman paid a similar tribute to Emerson. Whitman is thus of major importance in my study. Although as a mystic he takes a somewhat different path from that of Whitehead, both are alike in embracing a realistic as well as a mystic point of view.

This little volume begins and ends with Wordsworth as an exponent of much that Whitehead stands for in his concept of the lure for feeling. So convincing is the evidence for Wordsworth's influence on Whitehead that it cannot be dismissed as mere conjecture. Much that is implicit in Wordsworth is explicit in Whitehead.

In all but the first of these studies, which serves as a prelude to those that follow, my underlying purpose has been to reach a clearer understanding of Whitehead's metaphysical theories. As Whitehead finds much in Platonism that is in accord with the philosophy of organism and seeks to do justice both to monism and to pluralism, one may glimpse in these essays an attempt to show that romantic transcendentalism is not wholly at variance with science, nor mysticism or idealism with modern realism. Whitehead's basic principles may indeed be applied to all experience: philosophy for him including both science and religion, the latter being closely allied with art. In linking Whitehead with Goethe, Wordsworth, and Emerson, the aesthetic must be given special emphasis; and in connecting him with John Burroughs, in whose lifetime atomic theories were expanding, further consideration seems necessary of Whitehead's scientific views. That the conclusions of science are inextricably involved with the metaphysical has been admitted from Goethe through Whitman to Whitehead; and the claim of these thinkers that "an inner awareness" gives impetus to the creative drive was reiterated in 1957 by Arthur Compton.[3] Other scientists have indicated that if a deterministic mechanism cannot be applied to psychology or to the mental life, there must be "something in us," according to Sir Thomas Browne, "that can be without us and will be after us."[4]

In the preparation of these studies, I wish to acknowledge the assistance of Professor Derk Bodde of the University of Pennsylvania, Professor Filmer S. C. Northrop of Yale, Professor Victor Lowe of Johns Hopkins, and Professor William Ernest Hocking, Emeritus of Harvard. All four read with helpful comments portions of my work.

For encouragement in this project and useful suggestions I am grateful to a Wellesley classmate, Eloise Lownsbery Clancy, to Mrs. Elizabeth Hodder, Wellesley Professor Emeritus, to Professor Hoxie Fairchild of Hunter College, to Mrs. Anne M. Trinsey, formerly Dean at Hunter College Centre in the Bronx, and to Mr. Lucien Price, recorder of *Dialogues with Whitehead*. To Regina Adler, a former student of mine at Hunter, I am grateful for constructive assistance in documentation. For time given to critical comment on parts of the book, I would give special thanks to Mrs. Elizabeth Robinson Woods. I have been fortunate indeed in the privilege of conversations with Mrs. Alfred North Whitehead.

For the inclusion of the first and last studies in this volume, I am indebted to the courtesy of the *Journal of the History of Ideas* and of the *Journal of the Philosophy of Science*, in which the articles appeared in 1949 and 1956 respectively. My use in Chapter III of unpublished material on file at the Houghton Library of Harvard College has been kindly approved by Edward W. Forbes in behalf of the Emerson Memorial Association. Among libraries where I have worked, I would mention especially that of Bowdoin College and the gracious aid of its library staff.

M. A. W.

CONTENTS

THE LURE FOR FEELING

ANIMA MUNDI
IN CHINESE MYSTICISM AND IN WORDSWORTH

In an appreciation of Chinese Art, Olin Downes once called attention to the "unheard melodies" of a landscape scroll. It showed, he said, "an awareness of the world's wonder" that must lie at the root of all great art whether it be in the field of music, of poetry, or of painting.[1] Such an awareness led early Chinese poets and painters, as well as Wordsworth at a far later period, to acquaint themselves with the natural world, "to consider her ways and be wise." In the Orient and Occident alike it was a pantheistic mysticism[2] that found expression in poetry and art—a feeling of direct relationship with a unifying spirit of the universe. Contemporaries of Wordsworth in Europe and in America reflected a similar insight into the natural world including man; but the parallels to Chinese feeling and thought are in Wordsworth the closest and the most persistent.[3]

The conception of one life flowing through all, which critics have discussed more frequently perhaps than any other idea of Wordsworth's nature poetry,[4] is a basic theme also in the treatment of man and nature by Chinese sages and artists. They had drawn their inspiration from three streams of influence which blended in the Sung period (A.D. 960-1278), when poetry and art came to full flower, in the prevailing philosophy of Neo-Confucianism. These three streams of thought were to be found in the principles of Taoism, the discipline of Ch'an Buddhism,[5] and the classics of Confucius. Chu Hsi (1130-1200), who was the great synthesizer of Neo-Confucianism, was no more than Wordsworth a complete mystic. To him as to Wordsworth the natural world was an enduring, though changing reality: not in the Buddhist sense an illusion or apparition. Both, however, believed in a supreme, all pervading power unifying all life; and both believed in a principle above and beyond the natural world. To Chu Hsi this was the Supreme Ultimate;[6] to Wordsworth it was God. Their views of the universe might be called dualistic, but inclined toward monism and included a dynamic concept of nature resembling pantheism.

In their idea of a spiritual energy pervading nature Chu Hsi and Wordsworth showed not only a pantheistic approach to the universe, but a speculative or philosophic mysticism which seeks unity in cosmic activity. And in their attitude toward man and the universe we find evidence of their belief in the unity of *all* existence, which is a basic tenet of mysticism. The Neo-Confucian assumption that "all things are already complete in us"[7] parallels Wordsworth's concept of "the one life within us and abroad." In Chu Hsi's theory of knowledge as in Wordsworth's idea of perception there is implied an intimate relationship of man to the universe like that of microcosm to macrocosm. "When the mind is enlarged," says Chu Hsi, "it can enter into everything throughout the Universe." Then, "let the mind go so that it may be broad and tranquil and it will be enlarged."[8] "How exquisitely," Wordsworth muses, "the individual mind . . . to the external World is fitted . . . and how exquisitely too . . . the external World is fitted to the mind."[9]

There is sufficient evidence that both Chu Hsi and Wordsworth supported the mystical doctrine of unity in all life. Some reliance on intuition, by means of which mystics seek the truth, may also be seen in their approach to knowledge. Chu Hsi's method of investigating things Professor Hocking has called "response and penetration," the functioning of the mind resembling Bergson's idea of intuition[10] and being analogous to the "happy stillness of the mind" with which Wordsworth received the truth and the "energy" which he used in seeking it.[11] Professor Hocking finds Chu Hsi's "scnsc of consciousness throughout the universe" in more definite agreement with Whitehead,[12] whose appreciation of Wordsworth is also concerned with his sensitivity to the "presences" of nature and to their interpenetration.[13] A sense of harmony or equilibrium common to nature and man would thus seem to be suggested both in Chu Hsi and in Wordsworth,[14] and also an acceptance of intuition as a way of enlightenment. Both too would learn of nature through mental penetration of the object contemplated. To these tendencies of thought must be added aesthetic appreciation, which was particularly strong both in the Oriental and in Wordsworth, their mysticism being rooted in the senses.[15] All these factors entered into their awareness of unity in all existence, which is the main basis of comparison in this investigation.[16]

Before discussing further parallels in the approach to the universe of Wordsworth and his Oriental predecessors, certain distinct differences might be noted in their attitudes. The World Spirit or beneficent God of love inherited by Wordsworth from Christian tradition and from eighteenth century poets and philosophers is quite unlike the detached and impersonal force called in Chinese philosophy the Supreme Ultimate. Nor is there any parallel in Wordsworth's poems to such use of the supernatural by the Chinese as their fairies and genii mingling with the grander aspects of nature or their dragon, a symbol of natural and spiritual power quickening man to action. To the English poet's association of individual energy with active faith in immortality

> . . . hope that can never die,
> Effort and expectation and desire,
> And something evermore about to be.[17]

one finds little correspondence in Oriental thought.[18] The pantheistic approach to the universe by the Chinese is more objective and impersonal than that made by pantheistic poets of the West. Chu Hsi's interest in the physical world is more scientific and less sentimental than that of Wordsworth. In Chinese poetry one rarely finds as in Wordsworth's poems on small natural objects a moral appended. A didactic element is less apparent in the Oriental poet, and spiritual meaning is conveyed more subtly through suggestion.

As the Neo-Confucian system of thought represents a blending of three philosophies, the parallels between Wordsworth and the Chinese will be more clearly understood by first tracing the development of Chinese thought from the early sources of Neo-Confucianism in Taoism and Ch'an Buddhism.

The essence of Taoism may be found in the *Tao Te Ching*,[19] ascribed to Lao Tzu and literally translated by Arthur Waley as *The Way and its Power*.[20] The main tenet of Taoism entering into Chu Hsi's system of creation and corresponding in some degree to Wordsworth's conception of one life flowing through all:

> A motion and a spirit, that impels
> All thinking things, all objects of all thought,
> And rolls through all things. . . .[21]

is expressed in reference to the Tao itself, the Way, all pervading, and inexhaustible, interpreted as the all-embracing principle whereby all things are produced spontaneously rather than purposively.

> For the Way is a thing impalpable, incommensurable
> Incommensurable, impalpable,
> Yet latent in it are forms.[22]

The inter-relations of man and nature are particularly stressed with emphasis on the qualities that man may acquire if he lives in harmony with nature and its basic laws. Among these qualities are simplicity, humility, and calm quietude. Inherent in the thought of the Chinese and of Wordsworth is the idea of man and nature in spiritual rapport. To a mind that is still Lao Tzu says, "the whole universe surrenders."[23] And this stillness of mind Wordsworth finds coming from nature to man:

Nor less I deem that there are Powers
Which of themselves our mind impress;
That we can feed this mind of ours
In a wise passiveness.[24]

With such enlightenment, according to the *Tao Te Ching*,
comes also the assurance of immortality, but of one unlike
that of the Christian tradition in being impersonal.

Tao is forever and he that possesses it,
Though his body ceases, is not destroyed.[25]

Another body of Taoistic writing to which sages as well
as poets and painters in China were perhaps even more
indebted than to the *Tao Te Ching* is the work of Chuang
Tzu of the fourth and third centuries B.C. Again and again
we find in his philosophy ideas that suggest Wordsworth. To
the Chinese and to the English poet a sense of beauty in
the physical world is associated with the feeling of man's
relation to nature,[26] Chuang Tzu affirms that "the true Sage,
taking his stand upon the beauty of the Universe, pierces
the principles of created things." "The true Sage," he adds,
"performs nothing, beyond gazing at the Universe (In the
hope of attaining by contemplation, a like spontaneity).[27]
In the well-known "Lines Composed a Few Miles Above
Tintern Abbey" Wordsworth reiterates the feeling of Chuang
Tzu in the presence of nature:

While with an eye made quiet by the power
Of harmony, and the deep power of joy,
We see into the life of things.

The principles of quietness or wise passiveness, toler-
ance, and simplicity recommended in the *Tao Te Ching* are
repeated by Chuang Tzu; and throughout his writings he
stresses the thought of one life in all. Like the English poet
who on Mt. Snowdon sees the moon as an emblem of higher
minds feeding on infinity, he finds the highest level of

human existence in harmony with creation and in the becoming of one with the infinite.[28] Chuang Tzu designates this union of the individual with the universe as a state of pure experience. The spirit reaching this state then becomes an emptiness receptive to all truth, and freed from all fettering desires, attains absolute freedom. Wordsworth's explanation of intellectual love identified with the imagination is somewhat similar. To him it means "clearest insight, amplitude of mind, and reason in her most exalted mood." It also is associated with human freedom.[29]

Reflection of the Chinese spirit that is in harmony with creation may be seen in early Taoist poetry of the fourth century A.D. In "The Valley Wind," for instance, Lu Yün, the poet, retiring from society, becomes conscious of his kinship with the natural world.

> Living in retirement beyond the world,
> Silently enjoying isolation,
> I pull the rope of my door tighter
> And stuff my window with roots and ferns.
> My spirit is tuned to the Spring-season;
> At the fall of the year there is autumn in my heart.
> Thus imitating cosmic changes
> My cottage becomes a Universe.[30]

Wordsworth wrote in a similar vein of his reaction to the natural scenery of the Alps;

> Finally, whate'er
> I saw, or heard, or felt, was but a stream
> That flowed into a kindred stream.[31]

Such a feeling for nature was particularly strong in China during the T'ang dynasty, when poetry flourished as in no other period of Chinese history, and anticipated the great art of the Sung period. In this Golden Age Taoism found favor with Confucianists at court, who gave prestige to the philosophy of romantic mysticism expressed in poetry and in some landscape painting. The poets' approach to nature as the "soul of things" rooted in ancient Taoist principles, owed much also to the mystic vision of the Buddhist, particularly that of Mahayana Buddhism from which Ch'an Buddhism developed. The Mahayana doctrine of the void, that nothing was real apart from the whole, may have had an influence on later landscape painting. By the end of the seventh century Ch'an or Zen Buddhism was winning many followers and bringing a new vitality to the principles of Taoism.[32] To the romantic love of the Taoist for a universe in flux, a love sometimes combined with idleness and self-indulgence, Ch'an Buddhism contributed discipline in further development of will-power and self-control.[33] Men must look within as well as without to become attuned to the universal mind, but more emphasis was placed upon the necessity of action. If wisdom came in a flash through intuition after prolonged meditation, this sudden enlightenment might mean realization of one's vision through artistic accomplishment. By the eighth century painters as well as poets in China were influenced by the concepts of Ch'an Buddhism; they agreed with this philosophy and with Taoism in their emphasis on the rhythm and unity of being.[34] Poet painters equally skilled in the two arts have indeed made use of their gifts in the Orient to a degree unparalleled in other parts of the world. Many Chinese poems might be visualized as paintings; and in many a Chinese landscape one might find inspiration for a poem. Artists, in fact, frequently used specific poems for their themes in painting landscapes.

The two arts were evidently linked in Wordsworth's mind; he once wrote Sir George Beaumont that "it was impossible to excel in landscape painting without a strong tincture of the poetic spirit."[35] Wordsworth seems to have had definite ideas regarding the treatment of landscape in art;[36] and his appreciation of it was undoubtedly influenced by his own skill in landscape poetry. No one familiar with the pictures of mountain, lake, and forest scenery that abound in *The Prelude* and *The Excursion,* and form the subjects of many shorter poems, would disagree with Ruskin's assertion of Wordsworth's preeminence as a poetical

landscape painter.[37] The predominance of natural scenery in
his poetry helps to explain the analogues that may be found
to poetry and painting in China when those arts were at
the peak of their development.

Such a development appeared in the Sung period, which
was dominated by the Neo-Confucian philosophy[38] briefly
treated at the beginning of this study. As we return to this
system of thought, we may observe how Chu Hsi's theory
of creation substantiates his concept of one life in all. From
the existence of a universal law in all animate and inanimate life there comes a sense of unity in all being. This
universal law or principle is the Supreme Ultimate and contains within itself the laws governing the alternating movement and quiescence of the positive and negative ethers
yang and *yin* from whose union all separate objects in the
universe are formed. In all of these created entities including man exist separate laws making the created forms what
they are; and each and all of these laws exist first in the
Supreme Ultimate. Transcendent and above all earthly concepts, the Supreme Ultimate exists in man and in other
entities not only as separate laws but as a complete self;
and this self is reflected like "the moon in ten thousand
streams" in all phenomenal life.[39] Chu Hsi owed his theory
of creation chiefly to his immediate predecessors in the
Neo-Confucian school,[40] which started at the beginning of
the T'ang dynasty.[41] Although his system is a dualism, the
inter-relations he shows between matter and spirit point
toward a unity of being consistent with the main development of Chinese thought.[42]

No parallel to Chu Hsi's complicated theory of creation
may be found in Wordsworth's thinking.[43] We have already
suggested, however, that the awareness of unity in all existence felt by the Chinese philosopher and the English
poet was related to their sense of beauty and equilibrium
in the universe and to their belief in the attainment of
knowledge through penetration and through intuition. These
attitudes as well as a deep love for nature are indicated in
Neo-Confucian philosophy. In "The Doctrine of the Mean,"
equilibrium is called "the great root from which grow all

the human actings of the world."[44] In "The Great Learning," a sense of unity in man and nature is reflected in lines quoted from the *Shih Ching*, the earliest extant collection of Chinese poetry: "Lofty is that southern hill, with its rugged masses of rocks! Greatly distinguished are you, O grand-teacher Yin, the people all look up to you."[45] On the question of knowledge by penetration and by intuition we may read in "The Doctrine of the Mean" that the sage who can apprehend "without the exercise of thought" must first have studied, inquired about, reflected on, discriminated, and practiced "what is good."[46] Unlike the theory of wise passiveness in Taoism, Chu Hsi's interpretation of the extension of knowledge by intense application to the investigation of things, is in line with the disciplined search for enlightenment in Ch'an Buddhism. Wordsworth's substitution in his "Ode to Duty" of sterner discipline for wise passiveness parallels in his own thinking two characteristic points of view in the two philosophies. In the Neo-Confucian theory of complete enlightenment, a state of absolute sincerity bordering on the mystical[47] and influenced by Buddhism,[48] there is the nearest resemblance to Chuang Tzu's emphasis on becoming one with infinity. In both cases, as in Wordsworth's representation of a mind "that feeds upon infinity,"[49] the highest level of man's existence appears to be in harmony with creation.

In initiating his eclectic school of thought Chu Hsi combined, as we have suggested, the Taoist love of nature and the Ch'an Buddhist's search for enlightenment with his own interpretation of the Confucian classics. In view of this background it is not surprising to find Chu Hsi an eminent patron of art,[50] for the ideas in Neo-Confucianism or in earlier philosophies blended with it motivated many of the nature poems and landscape paintings of the T'ang and Sung eras. The poetry and painting of the two periods may then be considered together rather than chronologically as it is the philosophy entering into the creation of these Chinese poems and landscapes that is analogous to Wordsworth's treatment of nature. The discussion of poetry and painting that follows will begin with illustrations of the general theme of one life flowing through all and will proceed from representations of animism and of nature as a spiritual influence to poetic and artistic suggestions of mystic experience. In the examination of Wordsworth's thinking we pass gradually from the exaltation of nature to the apotheosis of man. Similarly in the consideration of Neo-Confucian ideas we conclude with the noble sage, investigating the laws of things mirrored in his own nature. He attains through simplicity and complete sincerity the height of human perfection and becomes the co-equal of earth and heaven.[51]

Strikingly similar in purport to that of nature poetry and painting in China is the poetry of Wordsworth expressing the idea that one life flows through all being. It was an idea that he never rejected. In *The Excursion* he called this pervasive spirit

> An active principle—howe'er removed
> From sense and observation, it subsists
> In all things, in all natures, in the stars
> Of azure heaven, the unenduring clouds,
> In flower and tree, in every pebbly stone
> That paves the brooks, the stationary rocks,
> The moving waters, and the invisible air.
> Whate'er exists hath properties that spread
> Beyond itself, communicating good,
> A simple blessing, or with evil mixed;
> Spirit that knows no insulated spot,
> No chasm, no solitude; from link to link
> It circulates, the Soul of all the worlds.[52]

The idea of motion or force behind all being,[53] which occurs not only here but in shorter poems such as "Lines Composed a Few Miles Above Tintern Abbey" and "A Slumber did my Spirit Seal," clearly resembles the Chinese concept of a universal rhythm of life, which is indicated more frequently possibly in their painting than in their poetry. It was the function of the artist to show in his landscapes the operations of spirit described in the *Book of*

Changes as the spirit of heaven and earth giving life to all visible being.[54] In the landscape poetry scattered through Wordsworth's *Prelude* and *Excursion* there is a mystical sense of a unifying or dynamic presence underlying natural beauty. Every element of the scene at sunrise,[55] for instance, when he dedicates himself to be a poet, contributes to the joyous spirit which breathes through the "sweetness of a common dawn": the laughing sea, the bright clouds, and the mountains "drenched in empyrian light."

To be alone with nature in order to become aware of the central unity of life was as essential to the poet Wordsworth as it was to the Sung painters. A feeling for solitary places brought to many a Chinese artist or poet the sense of his relation to infinity and motivated some of the finest T'ang poems and Sung landscapes.[56] Professors Havens and Sperry have both emphasized solitude as conditioning Wordsworth's belief in the underlying unity of the universe.[57] Loneliness Professor Sperry notes as the poet's device "for discovering his kinship with the natural world."[58] In another of Wordsworth's magic passages in *The Prelude* we feel that inner harmony which he found in all being. High up and alone in the hills of Grasmere his senses and imagination respond to the fusion of wind and rain and mist with the familiar elements of mountain scenery.

And afterwards the wind and sleety rain,
And all the business of the elements,
The single sheep, and the one blasted tree,
And the bleak music from the old stone wall,
The noise of wood and water, and the mist
That on the line of each of those two roads
Advanced in such indisputable shapes;
All these were kindred spectacles and sounds
To which I oft repaired, and thence would drink
As at a fountain.[59]

In an equally lonely spot a Chinese poet of the T'ang period had felt a mystic union in the rhythm of being. Visiting a Taoist priest far from civilization, Liu Changch'ing (graduating 733 A.D.) recorded briefly the beauties of the out-door world linked together in primal unity.

> Walking along a little garden path
> I found a footpath in the moss
> A white cloud low on the quiet lake
> Grasses that sweeten an idle door,
> A pine grown greener with the rain,
> A brook that comes from a mountain source
> And mingling with truth among the flowers,
> I have forgotten what to say.[60]

Lines written by Su-Tung-p'o (1036-1110) show a famous Sung poet feeling this same sense of identity in all existence:

> When the night is dark, all nature is in harmony,
> And man and beast are one.
> Substance and shadow allied, alone I stand enchanted.[61]

Such a sensitive identification of the artist with the universe motivated great landscape painting of the Sung period. The Sung painter sought to represent in his landscape the idea of a unifying spiritual presence.[62] For long periods he contemplated the grandeur of mountains and waterfalls in solitude before putting brush to paper.[63] Wonder merged with aesthetic and spiritual awareness as he lost himself in the beauty of the landscape. Like Wordsworth in preparing for creative activity, he freed his spirit from distracting desires by entering into the scene he contemplated. Using his mind as a mirror of the natural world he saw beyond mere beauty and with "clearest insight" caught the spiritual essence of the landscape.

The Sung painter would not copy nature; he would idealize it. In this attitude he resembled Ch'an Buddhists whether or not he followed their philosophy. The intuitive mind, we are told in the *Lankāvatāra Sutra*, is a link between the personal mind [in Locke's sense] and the universal mind.[64] Seeking enlightenment that would put him in harmony with the universe, the artist attempted to find in outward forms of nature symbols of the divine power or energy sustaining all life—an essence difficult for the mind to comprehend and more difficult to present in pictorial art. In consequence the great Sung landscapes are characterized by an ethereal quality called by artists of the period "spirit resonance" or the "reverberation of the universe,"[65] and recognized as the first canon of art.

Wordsworth's imagination rooted in the senses is identified through intuition with the World Soul. To him as to Chinese poets and painters, intuition was frequently a greater spur to the imagination than direct observation; and his mystic vision pierced the world of the senses. In its visible forms he found, as he said in *The Prelude*, "types and symbols of Eternity." This approach to nature is illustrated clearly in the second book of *The Prelude*.

Oft in these moments such a holy calm
Would overspread my soul, that bodily eyes
Were utterly forgotten, and what I saw
Appeared like something in myself, a dream,
A prospect in the mind.[66]

Chinese landscape painters represented this mystic attitude toward the world in a variety of ways. They suggested infinite energy streaming through all forms of being by rhythmical flowing brush strokes—a technique leading critics to compare Chinese painting to music.[67] The dynamic character of the brush strokes was acquired through practice in calligraphy, which had a great influence on Chinese painting.[68] Monochrome instead of color was applied in the finest landscapes as an appeal to the imagination rather than to the eye. The intuition of Ch'an Buddhism carried over into art was seen particularly in the economy of brush strokes: the indication of a stream by a few ripples, the bare outlining of sails and boats, and the use of empty spaces. The observer, in other words, was expected to discern more than met the eye. The painter's idea of the significance of a vacuum was due possibly in some degree to the concept of ether in the Neo-Confucian philosophy. Space, according to Chu Hsi, was filled with life-producing ether.[69] Why should it not then seem all embracing and mysterious to the artist, dominating phenomenal being as the greater part must always control the less.[70] As already intimated, empty spaces were used to suggest infinity; a similar illusion was created by a careful gradation of tones, a series of thin veils of haze or mist.[71]

This mystic attitude toward the natural world is suggested in a Chinese landscape painting of the twelfth century by the Sung artist, Ma Yüan (1198-1224). Rhythmical brush strokes indicating universal harmony of being show the winding shores of a stream and two willows bent and twisted by the elements but sending out branches that droop in graceful curves over the water. Their slender shoots appear to be swaying slightly in the breeze as the mist dissolves in the valley. Nearby a bridge spans the stream and leads to a village at the base of the mountains. In the background the ridges rise to precipitous heights and end at the sky line in rounded contours or in thin veils of mist. Laurence Binyon has identified the mood of tranquil and quiet joy in this scene with the spirit of Wordsworth's "Lines Written in Early Spring."[72] Most nearly allied perhaps to the feeling evoked by the painting is the sense of joy attributed to nature in the following verses:

> The budding twigs spread out their fan
> To catch the breezy air;
> And I must think, do all I can,
> That there was pleasure there.

This is one of many poems by Wordsworth showing in the treatment of nature a personifying tendency closely related to pantheism. In the work of Kuo Hsi (circa 1021-1090), an earlier painter than Ma Yüan, there is a clearer expression of animism. Mr. Sirén has pointed to a "mountain enthroned like an emperor," "stones like squatting tigers by the roadside," and "homegoing clouds," as elements in his landscapes that illustrate pantheism.[73] A similar animism was common among the Chinese poets of the T'ang period. Tu Fu (712-770), who on account of his intimate association with nature was called "the guest of rivers and lakes," gives to mountains at dawn human attributes.

> Clear sunrise, South of Ch'u Palace;
> Frost in the air, ten thousand mountain ranges hold it in their lips.[74]

And in a line expressing joy at a younger brother's visit,

> Reaching the eaves, twined together, plum flowers smile[75]

he is closely akin to Wordsworth in an earlier stanza of the poem cited

> And 'tis my faith that every flower
> Enjoys the air it breathes.

Supporting the theme of one life flowing through all, a spiritual influence in nature working on human character has been noted. Frequent illustrations of such a relationship may be found in Chinese poetry of the T'ang dynasty and in Wordsworth. In the work of Meng Hao-jan (689-740), a recluse poet, and in that of his friend Li Po (705-762), the most famous Taoist of the T'ang period, are lines showing spiritual effects of natural elements. Meng Hao-jan writes from the mountain lodge of a Buddhist priest:

> And now through pine-trees come the moon and chill of evening,
> And my ears feel pure with the sound of wind and water. . . .[76]

Li Po addresses a Buddhist friend in a mountain dwelling, saying:

> The pine tree shakes your garment
> And the stony brook cleanses your soul,
> How I envy you, who unperturbed
> Are pillowed high in a mist of emerald.[77]

Spiritual growth through an habitual association with nature is a familiar theme in many of Wordsworth's shorter poems as well as in *The Prelude* and *The Excursion*. In "Resolution and Independence" the old leech gatherer, assured in spite of his infirmity, reflects an enduring spirit in keeping with the ways of the universe.

> Motionless as a cloud the old Man stood
> That heareth not the loud winds when they call
> And moveth all together if it move at all.

Nature's promises to Lucy in "Three Years She Grew" are in the true spirit of Taoism:

> And hers shall be the breathing balm,
> And hers the silence and the calm
> Of mute insensate things.

The ennobling influence of dwelling on mountain heights, illustrated by the shepherd in Wordsworth's *Prelude*,[78] is felt frequently in Li Po's poetry. After his thirtieth year he had left court and given himself up to the solace of nature, believing that in returning home to his roots or to nature, he would be enlightened with knowledge of the eternal. Repeating the question of the wayfarer,

> Why do I live among the green mountains?

Li Po replies,

> I laugh and answer not; my soul is serene;
> It dwells in another heaven and earth belonging to no
>   man.[79]

Painters as well as poets in China advocated such a return to nature. Kuo Hsi writes that "in times of tyranny and misrule it is natural for wise men to go to the hills and forests."[80] From the pine they might learn strength, from the willow pliancy, and from the plum blossom purity. The symbolic uses of nature made by painters were innumerable. "Noise and dust, bridles and chains," Kuo Hsi continues, "these are what man's nature is ever weary of. Haze and mists, saints and fairies—for these man's nature pines eternally. . . ."[81] The Taoist immortals who, tradition says, haunt inaccessible mountain peaks or float across the sea to far-off islands, are familiarly known as saints and fairies; they are naturally associated with infinity symbolized in Chinese landscapes by haze and mist. Wordsworth's lines

Our destiny, our nature, and our home
Is with infinitude, and only there,[82]

voice a yearning akin in some respects to that of his Chinese predecessors.

"A Bridge to the Infinite" is the name given by Mr. Sirén to a landscape scroll ascribed to Tung Yüan (late 10th century), an early Sung painter.[83] The soft quiet atmosphere of a day clearing in the valley is disclosed as veils of mist rise and dissolve in the upper regions of the mountains in the background. In contrast to the distinctness of the scene in the valley, the stream and hazy base or foothills of the mountains seem to melt into each other at the line of convergence. Microscopic figures of men on a promontory waiting for a ferry and of pilgrims approaching a temple at the base of a hazy gorge heighten the mystic impression of the grandeur and infinitude of nature. The feeling of mystery in landscape merging into infinity is evoked more frequently by later Sung painters whose work was definitely influenced by the ideas of Ch'an Buddhism.[84] Ma Kuei (circa 1150-1224), the brother of Ma Yüan, shows skill in the use of empty spaces expressing the boundlessness of nature in "Two Men in a Boat on an Evening

Lake."[85] Here the two figures in the small craft, the vast stretches of vacant space blotting out lake, shore, and any trace of vegetation, and the dim outline of mountain peaks in the distance suggest not only the sense of infinity but deep harmony between man and the universe.

This sense of harmony and the impulse to create came at times to Chinese poets and to Wordsworth by way of mystic experience. To the beauteous forms of nature, Wordsworth says, he owes this state of mind:

> . . . that serene and blessed mood,
> In which the affections gently lead us on,—
> Until, the breath of this corporeal frame
> And even the motion of our human blood
> Almost suspended, we are laid asleep
> In body, and become a living soul.[86]

Critics of Wordsworth have described such moments variously as trances or as brief periods of ecstasy and insight. The poet writes of this experience as of sudden enlightenment:

> All that took place within me came and went
> As in a moment; yet with Time it dwells,
> And grateful memory, as a thing divine.[87]

In Chinese poetry such experiences are suggested, though the penetration and ecstasy are less immediate and less subjective. Li Po appended lines to the picture screen of a Buddhist friend in appreciation of the landscape portrayed; its mountain peaks, lonely pines, waterfalls, and shining mist.

> Whoever looks on this

he wrote

> Loses himself in eternity;[88]

Mystic wonder or ecstasy in the presence of natural beauty is frequently attributed to hermits, monks, or fishermen, who may typify poets or sages, in lyric poetry of the T'ang period. The old fisherman alone in a sea of mist or disappearing in the river fog and becoming one with infinity appears in painting and in poetry.[89]

It is already clear that enlightenment follows the artist's mystic experience. Such an identification with the universe would be difficult to illustrate in Chinese painting. It is perhaps more correct to call this experience a preparatory step before the artist puts brush to silk. To the finest of the Sung painters this form of mysticism did not represent an escape from life or defeatism, Mr. Sirén writes, but exaltation in being able to transfer immediately to silk or paper what should be the realization of an intuitive vision, and in a sense creating like nature herself.[90] Another work by Ma Yüan, "A Moon-lit Night,"[91] suggests such a purpose; here the sage or poet observer seems to be the controlling figure, representing perhaps the mind of the painter who created the scene. Seated on a shelving terrace of rock in the foreground, the artist or philosopher looks out beyond the perpendicular cliff rising above him, and gazes at the moon gleaming down from a starless heaven. At one point the empty space used to express infinity is broken by the giant arm of a twisted pine thrust out from the rocky crags in which it is entrenched. Pines painted by Ma Yüan have been called "lean and strong as iron," and were associated by him with the young dragon ready to spring into action, thus like the pine symbolizing a potential spiritual power.[92] Here the twisted, rugged strength of the pine-tree suggests a similar concentrated force in the character of the sage-observer. Ma Yüan's preparation for this painting must have been a dynamic, not a passive, experience as he envisaged philosopher, possibly himself as creator, in spiritual union with the elemental forces of nature. Such a conception would bring to mind the Neo-Confucian sage who, having attained complete enlightenment through the mystical state of absolute sincerity, is made the co-equal of earth and heaven.

All embracing is he and vast, deep and active as a
fountain, sending forth in their due season his virtues.

All embracing and vast, he is like heaven. Deep and
active as a fountain, he is like the abyss. He is seen, and
the people all reverence him;[93]

The theme in Ma Yüan's work and its suggested association with the Neo-Confucian sage find an echo in Wordsworth's mature attitude toward being. As experience deep-
ened his perceptions, the capacity of the soul of man in its
highest development was to him a revelation of the Deity or
World Soul more truly than had ever been the face of
nature. His last book of *The Prelude* concludes with a symbolic picture of "a majestic intellect" feeding "upon infinity"
and deriving "from the Deity" "that glorious faculty that
higher minds bear with them as their own."

. . . and lo! as I looked up,
The moon hung naked in a firmament
Of azure without cloud, and at my feet
Rested a silent sea of hoary mist.
. . .
There I beheld the emblem of a mind
That feeds upon infinity, that broods
Over the dark abyss, intent to hear
Its voices issuing forth to silent light
In one continuous stream; a mind sustained
By recognition of transcendent power,
In sense conducting to ideal form
In soul of more than mortal privilege.[94]

Ignorant in all probability of the skill and purpose of the
Chinese landscape artists at the height of their development during the Sung dynasty, Wordsworth does yet suggest here an attitude toward man and the universe similar
to that which they sought to represent by the flowing
rhythm of their brush strokes in monochrome.

The conception of a world soul with varying implications has appeared so frequently in the history of mankind

regardless of time or place, of race or language, that to speculate on Chinese influence in Wordsworth's thinking would seem to be futile.[95] In conclusion then we would re-iterate that five hundred years and more before Words-worth, Chinese sages and artists, in their pantheistic and mystic theme of one life flowing through all, foreshadowed a European attitude toward nature and man that was to be particularly marked in our English poet. Certainly in their awareness of a spiritual force underlying the universe, in their theory of an animated nature and of the ennobling power of its influence, and in their contemplation of the Infinite to whom men may turn for wisdom, these Chinese sages, poets, and painters have with Wordsworth an indubitable kinship in feeling and thought.

II

THE LURE FOR FEELING
IN THE
PHILOSOPHY OF ORGANISM

An awareness of one life in all was in Chinese art and thought and in Wordsworth a lure for feeling. To the Chinese artist, it was spirit resonance or the breath of heaven that could be revealed symbolically in his landscape painting. To Wordsworth it was something deeply interfused throughout the natural world. Either concept involves a mystic element. Chu Hsi, representing the Neo-Confucianists, though of both Taoist and Buddhist persuasion, was more inclined to look for a rational interpretation of the universe. This was also the purpose of Alfred North Whitehead in developing his philosophy of organism. Yet the vision of the mystic supplemented his scientific and philosophical speculations, particularly in the rôle he assigned to the *lure for feeling.* In his organic theories the lure appears in various guises, but is mainly allied with God in the world: God in his primordial, conceptual nature, guiding creation to order and value; and God in his consequent nature, embodying all values in the creative advance of the universe. In the guise of spirit, the lure, pervasive throughout the natural world including man, is first of all a persuasive power. With magnetic attraction, it leads a receptive being to action and to the realization of potentiality. How this is done is elaborated through many pages of Whitehead's *Process and Reality;* and one must recognize the danger of hazarding an explanation in a brief chapter; but potentiality as something inherent in the past and the present, and something else to be actualized in the possible future, is perhaps a fitting point of departure.

With this latent something available for development the

lure is particularly associated, and is thus seen in the essences of phenomenal things and of ideal qualities, which
have their source in Plato's ideas and are termed by Whitehead *eternal objects*. They are suggested in Wordsworth's
reflection on "universal power and fitness in the latent
qualities and essences of things."[1] Color is such an essence,
is timeless, something eternal, Whitehead says, that comes
and goes without reference conceptually to any known entity. But he adds that an eternal object actualized in the
material world may represent value potential for the becoming of further realities. For instance, the golden glow
radiating from a maple tree in an October sunset, is a color
that exists eternally quite apart from the tree. But that hue
of molten gold at sunset may absorb the attention of an
artist and later become a dominant element in his painting
of an autumn scene. Thus the maple tree in embodying color
as an eternal object becomes a lure in an enduring world of
value, which Whitehead designates as one phase of the
universe; the other phase, he notes as activity or change, in
which the lure, originating from the physical world derived from God, plays its rôle conceptually in beckoning
toward a potential future.

The whole business of process, which for Whitehead as
for Bergson is the essence of reality, is the actualizing of
potentiality as an ingredient in something real through the
guidance of the lure. The potentiality of the past is the
inflow of the material world, or the experience of a subject,
into process, as well as that subject's possession of inherited
qualities; new potential factors are added in the present,
involving the conception of eternal objects or ideals, some
being contrasting elements; but elements concerned with
the physical world and derivative ideas must grow together
in harmony following the lure until satisfaction is attained
with the termination of definite and private experience.
Through this achievement of value the experience then
leaves its imprint as a public fact or as objective immortality.

This actualization of potentiality as an ingredient in
something real might be illustrated by the experience of

Otto Lilienthal, pioneer inventor of the flying glider. Process here is obviously considered on a scale of some magnitude. The initial stage for him may be his preoccupation with winged creatures and their manner of flight—the inflow of the material world. The potentiality of the past probably includes for him also inherited mechanical and engineering ability. As process continues, we may imagine his concepts of gravity, equilibrium, and control intermingling with his observations on the flying of birds, possibly in part derived from them. The lure, which guides the how of feeling, would seem to be particularly associated with Lilienthal's novel belief in the superiority of a curved rather than a flat surface for the flight of machines heavier than air. Here also the element of contrast is introduced. A driving urge or purpose, which we ascribe to the persuasive power of the lure is intensified by contrasts, and results in the satisfaction of producing a flying glider covering distances up to 1000 feet. The glider then as a novelty passes into objective immortality; but its value in a material world has been chiefly its lure to further progress in the evolving of the airplane.

Objective immortality is a term which Whitehead identifies with permanence as well as value. Though this means to him literally the world in God or God in his consequent nature, the primordial nature of God as the basis of all order is not excluded. It is through His guidance as the lure for feeling that a balanced coordination of permanence and fluency is attained, progressing from private experience to public fact, and thus emerging from the self-enjoyment of one to join the many values in the universe that again may lend themselves to the becoming of further novelties. As an intermediary concerned with harmonious relations in the interweaving of elements of experience, the lure then is not out of line with recent interpretation of metaphysics. Gotschalk, for instance, suggests as fundamental in process, relation or structure serving as a ground from which the two co-ultimates, the continuant (persistence) and the event (change), arise.[2]

This principle that relation between permanence or pure

being and activity or change is fundamentally ultimate, is not however new, for it entered into philosophy as inter-relation between the one and the many before the time of Plato. The monists have stressed permanence or the One; the pluralists, change or the many. Whitehead in the twentieth century indicates the necessary connection between the two, and endeavors to do justice to both; but in stressing creativity and its multiplicity of occasions as ultimate, he takes his stand on pluralism. Through unceasing and infinite creation of events conditioned by God he sees the universe advancing. The one may be to him a living occasion or event arising from values in the material world, and developing in process; but in a larger sense the One is the primordial nature of God. Only as life participates in such transcendental being through the lure for feeling may there be achievement of value. This concept of God's direct relationship with his creatures gives to the lure a mystic character.

Professor Hocking has queried whether the Neo-Realists, with whom Whitehead has been at times identified, may not be regarding universal essences (or eternal objects) as a substitute for the Absolute Mind; thus they would represent a form of monism and justify his suggestion that they are "mystics in disguise."[3] Whitehead's constant protest against the self-sufficiency of substance is indeed akin to the mystic's assertion that separateness is unreal. In stressing process rather than fact Whitehead has admitted that his philosophy ". . . seems to approximate more to some strains of Indian, or Chinese, thought than to western . . . thought."[4] Certainly the ideas in Taoism of the rhythm of life and of the interdependence of all things bear some resemblance to his own theories. As early as 1919 he concluded his *Enquiry into the Principles of Natural Knowledge* with an emphasis on the importance of rhythm in weaving a pattern. Its essence as the fusion of sameness and novelty is indicated in greater detail in *Process and Reality* as he introduces the vector character of re-enacting through the lure in process.

In Chu Hsi's philosophy, sketched in the preceding study, process shows the influence of Taoism; and as in the philosophy of organism, there is necessary connection between the One and the Many. The Supreme Ultimate contains the law for each individual entity, and through these laws determines the form of all the myriad things in the universe. The relationship between the Supreme Ultimate, its laws, and the many things in the world, is somewhat similar to the relationship in the philosophy of organism between God, eternal objects, and actual entities. The relevance of objects to the many living entities or occasions is envisaged in the mind of God. It is through His guidance as the lure for feeling that the potentialities of these essences are realized in creativity that ends in value.

The lure then suggests purpose, and is in fact called by Whitehead the final cause. Purpose is an outstanding feature in the philosophy of organism. Susanne Langer quotes Whitehead in confirming her own connection of purpose with the idea of human freedom. "The essence of freedom," he notes, "is the practicability of purpose."[5] In higher phases of experience he sees all decision that ends in satisfaction made independently, though subject to the persuasive power of God. Purpose adds something of novelty to mere reproduction of inherited character modified by environment; and thus the aim of the experiencing subject in facing the future, links the efficient cause with the final cause, or the immanence of the past with the potentialities of the conceptual aim. Novelty and life are to Whitehead associated with purpose. Naturalistic and mechanistic philosophies recognize only the efficient cause; and to naturalism, positivism, or mechanism Whitehead is opposed. To him there is something more in the world than nature and the efficient cause. Aristotle sees God as the First and Final Cause toward which all things move. Whitehead sees God in his primordial nature acting as Final Cause. Through the lure for feeling he guides all things to Himself in his consequent nature. Thus God in the World moves toward the World in God.

The place of the lure for feeling in the philosophy of organism we have already glimpsed in its relation to potentiality through persuasive power, and in its mystic rôle as intermediary between permanence and flux in process. The objective and subjective nature of the lure has also been implied in its appeal to a subject's senses through the physical world, and to his mind or spirit through a derivative suggestion of novelty. Thus physical and conceptual experience illustrate Whitehead's theory that every entity or *living occasion* has a physical and mental pole.

Although it is only in *Process and Reality* that the lure is an explicit part of Whitehead's philosophy of organism, we are prepared for it in *Science and the Modern World*, where the idea of organism is firmly established. Here in Whitehead's view of God as the principle of concretion and of limitation, one may find a suggestion of the lure in its persuasive initiation of purpose and in its guidance to the realization of potentiality. Process itself, in which the lure like an "underlying eternal energy" leads to the unification of interacting elements, is the starting point of Whitehead's notion of an organism. The "emergence of organisms," he notes, "depends on a selective activity akin to purpose."[6]

In *Adventures of Ideas* the notion of the lure lingers in the urge of the soul toward perfection as represented by Plato's Eros. Whitehead's most significant reference to the lure, however, comes at the conclusion of *Process and Reality*, where he asserts, "God is the lure for feeling, the eternal urge of desire." God as the supreme example of a living entity, but also as the basis of all order, feels the urge toward universal creation. The lure is also felt in varying degrees by all his creatures. In the sense of unconscious aim, Whitehead indicates, it may be applied to all forms of life. It is seen in the plant that turns its leaves toward the sun; in lower forms of life, where it is the germ of mind; and in the motivating impulse of higher phases of experience as well as in the persuasive, primordial nature of God.[7] In human creativity the lure obviously awakens a sense of value for what is beyond. When conscious, it represents both aim and goal, the one through the various stages of process transformed into the other.

The anticipation of value for what is yet to be determined is one phase of *feeling,* a word used in a technical sense that covers many aspects of perception or the relation between subject and object. In expressing a subject's concern for a selected portion of the universe, the term *feeling* is synonymous with *positive prehension* or the appriation of data to serve as components of a subject's *concresence,* the growing together of its formative elements in the process of becoming. Important too is a *negative prehension* that eliminates incompatible elements from feeling. It should be already clear that feelings, in accordance with the idea of physical and mental poles in an occasion, may be *physical;* arising through the senses from the actual world, or *conceptual,* involving ideas derived from the actual world. Often feeling is a combination of the two types of prehension, and is called by Whitehead *hybrid* or *impure.* Examples of conceptual feeling are *appetition* and *valuation:* the first, awakening purpose and allied with God's immanence in the world, he has described as "an urge toward the future based on an appetite in the present."[8] Valuation is the *subjective form* or how of feeling, which in its decisions, purposeful or otherwise may increase or diminish intensity. Consciousness comes with intensity of feeling, with a comparison of what may be with what is not, or with a yes or no judgment on a proposition. The union of physical and conceptual prehensions is seen in comparative feelings, where the datum to be entertained as a lure for feeling may be a theory or a proposition. Feelings or prehensions of whatever type are subject to the persuasive power of the lure, and are causal links in the successive phases of concresence that should end in satisfaction. Feeling is thus a central factor in the process of becoming.

What in Whitehead's background may have contributed to his idea of the lure for feeling should perhaps be given early consideration in an attempt to interpret the meaning of his concept. Three influences come to mind that throw light on the lure as it functions in Whitehead's philosophy of organism: his delight in Greek philosophy, particularly that of Plato; his preoccupation with mathematics, especially as allied with physics; and his Christian heritage.

Stemming from Plato's universal forms are Whitehead's

eternal objects that we have seen to be basic in his scheme; apart from them the lure could hardly function in the philosophy of organism. Yet Whitehead shows definite divergence from Plato, whose forms, culminating as a hierarchy of ideals in the Good, do not exist in the world; it is rather their imitations on earth that shadow forth ideal reality. Whitehead would see the eternal objects incarnated in the actual things of the world in accordance with their relevance to these things in the primordial mind of God, who, in connection with creation, envisages the whole realm of eternal objects. As potentialities they are relevant in varying degrees, and thus the myriad forms of creation are distinguished. Compare, for instance, the shape of a lemon and an orange; the color of carmine and coral; the taste of a bon-bon and an olive; the smell of a rose and a lilac; the song of a thrush and an oriole; and the joy of a child over a new toy with that of a mother over her firstborn. Eternal objects, one sees, may be felt physically when they appeal to the senses through shape, color, taste, smell, and sound; or they may be felt conceptually when expressing emotional or spiritual qualities such as joy, fear, love, beauty, or harmony. Yet in defining an eternal object, Whitehead is thinking of it as an abstraction that may be recognized mentally without any necessary reference to temporal objects,[9] but as a link between God and the world.

Thus we have seen the distinguishing characteristics of entities in the actual world and in the world of ideas as envisaged in the mind of God. His conceptual nature gives to the world as He entertains eternal objects relevant respectively to his creatures as they become through process; His consequent nature, on the other hand, receives from the world the results of process that make for a stable, aesthetic order. The conceptual persuasiveness of God as a lure for feeling is supplemented then by the solicitude of his reception as consequent God. With a "tender care that nothing be lost" He may gather up what appears to be evil, foreseeing its ultimate value. For instance, the possible uses of atomic power for the good of mankind may outweigh its capacity for destruction.

For his idea of God Whitehead seems to be partially

indebted to Greek philosophy. Aristotle's metaphysical use of the phrase "object of desire" Whitehead finds in harmony with his own interpretation of God as the lure for feeling— the "eternal urge of desire"—initiating all creative activity.[10] But it would seem to be Plato who suggested to him the persuasive power of the lure in its urge toward perfection. In the *Sophist* and in the *Timaeus*, he finds references to a divine agency in the world that is persuasive and not coercive. Only in his later dialogues, Whitehead notes, does Plato produce such intermediaries as Demiurge and Eros: Demiurge as an auxiliary creator and Eros as love urging the soul toward perfection. Whitehead's interpretation of Eros throws light on the function of the lure as a guide to the soul or subject in the experience of one arising out of many. The subject we have seen attracted first by the physical world, then entertaining eternal objects or conceptual ideas suggested by the original data. The order of process from the material world to the mental or spiritual recalls the order in the Symposium as Eros ascends to heavenly love and beauty.

In Whitehead's insistence upon the immanence of God in the world acting as the lure for feeling, he considers himself diverging from what he believes to be the most consistent view of Plato's, the separation of God from his creatures. Regarding God as the principle of concretion and of limitation within the world, Whitehead had a very different point of view. Yet even here hints from *The Philebus* may have contributed to his thinking. The fusion of the finite with the infinite, two of Plato's divisions of temporal existence, must have given him pause, for the finite to Plato here means law or measure, and from the mixture of this limit with the infinite, the many indiscriminate entities in the universe, are generated all the good things of the earth. Thus the finite may have suggested Whitehead's idea of God as a principle of limitation, the eternal urge toward law and order and the good as separate from chaos and evil.

Through the principle of concretion Whitehead sees the animate world built up of living occasions or events, which appear in Plato as things or entities without the subject object relation; but the arising of one out of the composition of many is implied by a remark of Socrates in the *Theatetus:*

> . . . out of motion and change and admixture all things are becoming relatively to one another . . . ; and that which by uniting with something becomes an agent, by meeting with some other thing is converted into a patient. And from all these considerations, as I said at first, there arises a general reflection that there is no one self-existent thing . . . (Jowett's translation)

In the *Timaeus* Plato adds that an entity "is always in process of becoming and never really is," a phrase that Whitehead finds analogous to the modern concept of "an actual entity in a fluent world."[11] These two sources from Plato suggest two aspects of Whitehead's theory of process: a becoming resulting from successive series of integrations and a loss of actuality as process terminates in satisfaction. But Whitehead would give to eternal objects actualized in the world the power which Plato gives to universal forms as ideals to be imitated. Living occasions, Whitehead insists, retain their power of being through their objective immortality. The idea of objective immortality in personality, we may see illustrated in George Eliot's "choir invisible" ". . . of those immortal dead who live in minds made better by their presence." Such everlastingness serves as a lure in the becoming of the universe.

In talking of the lure, of eternal objects, and of God, we have been dealing with abstractions, but with abstractions that have a deep impact upon life—an impact that may be more fully understood by turning to mathematics, the study of inter-relations, which the Greeks in their time associated with deity. Measure and proportion Plato identifies with beauty and virtue, which come from God, with law and order exemplified in God, and with the degree or intensity of universal forms or essences shadowed forth in the world. As Whitehead seeks in metaphysics a satisfactory system, his early mathematical studies continue to influence his thought. To Plato in the *Timaeus,* the foundations of the universe are geometrical patterns. To Whitehead the world is made up of occasions, the units of process, and also, figuratively speaking, patterns. As an arc may become a circle by following mathematical law, may not then an experience or natural fact arrive at completion in the process of becoming, through the guidance or limitation of God as lure for feeling? Mathematics, as it functions in the world, would seem to resemble in some sort the functioning of Whitehead's eternal objects, which have value and actuality as they become ingredients in the generation of things; these things in turn are perceived through the ingredience of eternal objects.

Our knowledge of the universe has increased as abstract reasoning in the form of mathematical formulae has been used to interpret natural facts. Consider, for instance, the value of mathematics to Maxwell, to Planck, and to Einstein in their discovery of electro-magnetism, the quantum theory, and relativity. "Nothing is more impressive," Whitehead writes, "than the fact that as mathematics withdrew increasingly into the upper regions of ever greater extremes of abstract thought, it returned back to earth with a corresponding growth of importance for the analysis of concrete fact."[12] And as analysis of concrete fact is rendered possible by higher mathematics, perception of concrete facts is contingent upon ideal, eternal objects, whose relevance to actual things is determined by the abstract, primordial nature of God.

Whitehead's linking of natural laws with mathematics has taken us into the field of physics, which is closely associated with his speculative thought, and gives added meaning to his scientific theories of process. As early as 1905 he wrote an article on "Mathematical Concepts of the Material World." The idea of mutually exclusive entities of space, matter, and time, which Whitehead noted was entertained by the Greeks, he sees reflected also in Newton's belief that "mass remained permanent during all changes of motion"[13] and thus had the property of simple location. To this notion we find Whitehead constantly protesting. In this early paper his insistence on a changing universe is seen in his preference for Leibnitz's concept of a cosmos in which no part is exempted from change. Whitehead treats space here as a field of force in which his linear ultimates suggest electro-magnetic lines of force in their effect upon molecular and sub-molecular events. In summarizing the thought of this study, Professor Lowe notes that a particle or corpuscle is recognized as a volume "whose permanence is the persistence of some peculiarity of motion of linear ultimates passing through it," and in this respect resembles an earlier notion of a knot in the ether.[14] The electron as a bundle of lines absorbing and transmitting energy, illustrates a concresence of elements, which is a basic character of Whitehead's living occasions. The linear ultimates resemble vectors as carriers and transmitters of energy, and the electrons in their periodic vibrations are analogous to the reiteration or re-enaction of feeling in successive prehensions in occasions or events. Thus in their functioning, electrons and occasions would both appear to be examples of the primary entities making up the inorganic and organic universe. That there is an order of nature is Whitehead's firm belief; and this trend in European thought he considers basic in motivating scientific research. The very possibility of science, he sees in *Science and the Modern World*, unconsciously connected with the medieval idea, derived from tradition, of the rational nature of God.

So far we have seen possible suggestions from Greek philosophy and from science for Whitehead's ideas on process and the lure for feeling. He has found deficiencies in Plato's notions of God that are in one way corrected by the theism of his Christian heritage—his immediate background. As the son of an English vicar he knew the Bible well and was familiar with Christian theology. Though he turned away from much in both as his speculative philosophy developed, there was a basic principle which held him —perhaps because it seemed to supply what he found lacking in Greek metaphysics—the idea of immanence or of God in the world. Christian theologians, Whitehead points out, marked an important stage in thought when they

gave God a share in the nature of the world by their belief
in His incarnation in the one person of Christ and in His
immanence generally in the third person of the Trinity.[15] In
either case a "direct doctrine of immanence" is implied and
remains, Whitehead notes, as a significant metaphysical discovery. He sees in Plato's Psyche and Eros indwelling powers of persuasiveness luring the world to immortal love and
beauty; and he finds in Christ a persuasive agent pursuing
his desire for perfection through love, and in his victorious
life illustrating the lure for feeling, the eternal urge of
desire, by his own idea of creative advance—the building
of the kingdom of heaven upon earth. Plato's conviction of
a divine and persuasive agency in the world Whitehead
noted as a doctrine of importance in the history of religion,
but a doctrine improved upon by Christian theology in its
insistence on God's actual immanence in the world.

The vision of a new social order contemplated by Christ
as the kingdom of heaven upon earth, requires, according to
Whitehead, the inclusion of God in our secular thinking.
Thus in the philosophy of organism the primordial nature
of God exerts in every day affairs the lure or element of
persuasion. "The things which are temporal arise by their
participation in the things which are eternal."[16] The non-
temporal objects in turn acquire actuality by their ingression into life that is temporal. In this mediation between
the ideal and the concrete, the actual functioning of the
lure for feeling, Whitehead sees the working out of his
ontological principle and the development of process.

What seem to be important influences on the development of Whitehead's concept of God, of eternal objects,
and of process in their bearing on the lure for feeling have
been reviewed. Further light now may come from an examination of the lure's connection with Whitehead's ontological
principle and of its participation in the stages of process
and of feeling. Whitehead begins his discussion of process
by announcing his ontological principle, which he terms the
union of efficient and final causation, but he sums up the
principle in his conclusion that everything in existence has a
reason in the "composite nature" of other entities and in

God.[17] Efficient and final causation would seem to cover for
Whitehead the four causes of Aristotle. Aristotle's material
cause indicating the constituent elements of an entity, is to
Whitehead largely the efficient cause. The other three causes
of Aristotle are partially covered by Whitehead's final cause;
for instance, the sense of agency in Aristotle's efficient cause,
the evolving of a pattern in his formal cause, and the purpose in becoming of his final cause are all associated with
Whitehead's subjective aim, which emerges from his lure
for feeling, called by him the final cause.

Efficient and final causation are allied by Whitehead
with immanence and transcendence. To him every actual
entity has an indirect reason for existence in the environment of its actual world, which is defined by eternal objects; or it has a direct reason in the character of that
entity, whose transcendent, subjective aim comes from God.
The immanent and transcendent reasons for the becoming
of an occasion or entity are revealed in the two early stages
of process: first, mere receptivity of the physical world with
which the subject of the occasion or entity is concerned;
here what attracts the subject of the prehension is defined
by eternal objects that are actualized in the world; they are
in Whitehead's words "realized determinants." Following
this prehension is a more positive admission of the eternal
objects in the physical world as they suggest derivative
ideals with which they are joined in a possible theory or
proposition. Here the ideals or eternal objects entertained
are characterized by transcendence, having "a capacity for
determination." For example, flying creatures, particularly
the curvature of their wings, absorbed the attention of
Lilienthal, as noted in the early part of this chapter; and
their movements in flight suggested the possible construc-
tion of an air ship. The proposition, "It is possible to create
a flying glider," then became to him a lure for feeling. Thus
it is that the subjective aim emerges from the lure in the
transcendent phase of creativity.

For further illustration we might turn to the poetry of
Wordsworth, whose feeling for nature deeply impressed
Whitehead. Let the process in the mind of the poet be the

growth of Wordsworth's poem, "I wandered lonely as a cloud." In a solitary but receptive mood Wordsworth comes upon a host of daffodils swaying in the breeze by the margin of a bay. Their beauty and graceful motion have magnetic attraction for the poet, who now experiences the lure in the sense of appetition or an urge toward some value not yet existing.

> I gazed and gazed but little thought
> What wealth the show to me had brought

The positive impact upon his own mind of the daffodils "fluttering and dancing in the breeze" and outdoing the "dancing waves in glee" brings concentration on the emotional quality of the eternal objects suggested by the data he is prehending. The poet's insight and subjective aim are indicated as he finds in the host of blossoms "tossing their heads in sprightly dance" a picture of gaiety and joy in contrast to his own feeling of solitude. But the apparent contrasts are compatible, for

> A poet could not but be gay
> in such a jocund company

As the pattern or theme unfolds, the contrast of liveliness and joy with the loneliness of the poet's spirit, is reiterated in successive prehensions until in the final phase of unified satisfaction the recollection of the daffodils with a similar interaction of emotions, brings a thrill of pleasure as

> They flash upon the inward eye
> Which is the bliss of solitude.   .

The living occasion sketched here in bare outline lacks many technical details elaborated by Whitehead; but one may get a general idea of the lure's function in Whitehead's stages of process, and may see as well a resemblance to Plato's thought on the interaction of entities. To the subject of any occasion in process, Whitehead ascribes "the triple character of recipient, patient, and agent."[18] The poet's mental operations would be here the recipient subject responding to the lure or magnetic attraction of the daffodils in their setting. By uniting this physical prehension with the derived conceptual prehension of gaiety and joy, the subject might again find in a proposition such as "Gaiety and a solitary mood may be pleasurably combined" a lure for feeling. Guided by the lure to the subjective form or how of feeling, the subject could be both patient and agent. In the rôle of patient he would be submitting himself to persuasive power and be finding pleasure through contrasts. As agent he would be the controlling part of a concrescence in which elements may be dismissed as incompatible or accepted as compatible through harmony or by way of contrast. The composition of the poem completed, a novelty possessed of objective immortality is born into the world. Although Whitehead agrees with Plato that "all things are becoming relatively to each other," and that "there is no one self-existent thing," he finds in each occasion growing out of complexity "a singularity in being itself alone."

No statement could be more true of Wordsworth's poems on natural objects. His mental operations in composing the poem on the daffodils also suggest Whitehead's theories on process and the lure as derived from his interest in physics. In the vector field and in the quantum theory, for instance, Whitehead finds a tentative justification of his organic theories, particularly his speculations on vibratory existence. The initial prehension in the case of Wordsworth's poem has a vector character in the force with which the poet's appropriation or prehension of a portion of nature is carried from the shore of the bay to his own mind, then re-enacted with increasing intensity in successive prehensions. Entities objectified for prehension in a new occasion, Whitehead says, exert their power to attract not as separate things but as a unit. And it was the conjunction of daffodils swaying in the breeze beneath the trees with the dancing waves of the bay that caught the poet's absorbed attention. So viewed, Whitehead remarks in *Adventures of Ideas*, objects ". . . carry the creativity which drives the world."[19]

Whitehead makes the function of the lure in process clearer through his discussion of the conformal, conceptual, and comparative phases of feeling. The first two stages of conformal and conceptual feelings are in fact similar to physical and conceptual prehensions, both involving a response that may be unconscious. It may be appetition or incipient valuation such as kept Wordsworth gazing at the daffodils, hardly aware of the enrichment of his experience. The question of the unconscious and the conscious, Whitehead indicates, is determined more or less by the power of the lure to evoke intensity. Valuation up or down in the simplest character of conceptual feeling may be unconscious; but as valuation includes intellectual operations, it becomes conscious. This is particularly true of comparative feelings which introduce the complexity of theories or propositions. For example, when the lure for feeling is a proposition involving an affirmative or negative reaction, valuation may become a conscious judgment.[20]

For Whitehead "consciousness is the crown of experience ... not its necessary base";[21] unconsciousness he regards as deeply significant, for it is prior to consciousness and represents totality of experience whereas consciousness is involved in a selection of events. Day dreams, mental activity in sleep, and much of the conceptual feeling that prompts action is unconscious; but the conscious must include recollection, and may result, Whitehead intimates, in a sudden awareness of a situation that has been built up little by little. Consciousness may then present a contrast between what is and what might be, and may thus evoke intensity of feeling.

Whitehead might have seen an illustration of such an experience in the predicament of Isabel Osmond at the end of *The Portrait of a Lady* as she faces a future which she must determine in part for herself. Through an accumulation of memories consciousness flares up in a shock of recognition as she sees herself the victim of her husband and his mistress, who would use her for their own ends. Intensity of feeling mounts as she realizes the contrast between what her marriage might be and what it is, and decision becomes imperative as to her own position in the present and in the immediate future. The lure for feeling then in conscious experience may be an ideal of conduct, expressed possibly as a proposition and emerging as the final cause.

Consciousness in its sudden awareness is linked inextricably by Whitehead with spontaneity and art. The aesthetic experience is an evocation of intensities from a realization of contrast under identity. Art to him follows his theory of process; all order is indeed aesthetic order. "The actual world is the outcome of aesthetic order."[22] A confirmation of this theory may be seen in the Chinese idea of creativity, involving the union of *Yang* and *Yin*—the contrast of heaven and earth or of spirit and matter. "Aesthetic experience," Whitehead notes, "comes from the immanence of God"—a phase of the lure for feeling. The possible experience of an artist may help in clarifying his concepts.

Let us imagine an artist watching the sunrise from a rocky point on the sea coast. Before him are dark green spruce trees silhouetted against the crimson sky and the deep blue of the sea; gray rocks of myriad shapes take on from the heavens a rosy hue; and tree-fringed islands emerge here and there from the expanse of waters between the point and the distant horizon. Into the artist's mind comes a feeling of unrest, a zest to achieve "what is not and yet may be" through the drawing power of the lure. Out of this *appetition* as termed by Whitehead emerges a subjective aim, to be followed by a determined subjective form, or how of feeling, in the painting of a picture, the transforming in the mind of the artist of what is before him. As the subjective aim gains intensity, it becomes absorbed awareness involving consciousness. In this process God as the principle of limitation may be functioning. A satisfying transformation of what the artist sees will come through the weighing and balancing of eternal objects derived from the scene before him, in their transcendent potentiality. Not only colors and shapes, but conceptual or emotional qualities must enter the picture. Is it tranquility or sensation, charm or majesty that he should emphasize? The process of composition is a part of the artist himself, and when completed perishes, enduring only if it has value by reaching perfection as a painting. The elements to be represented on canvas coalesce in harmony. Colors and shapes may contrast or blend, but the unifying eternal objects, the emotional impact of the scene, its possible glory and majesty, bring together as one sky and sea, trees and rocks, and tiny islands against the far horizon, the rim of the world. Thus the painting, if it catches this ideal beauty, achieves objective immortality, and from subject in the making becomes object to serve in further enriching of experience.

Whitehead's interpretation of appearance and reality reveals the process by which the lure, arising from a rich and varied background of reality—"stubborn facts" enduring through their objective immortality—is concentrated on distinct elements in the subject's environment, and by simplifying and intensifying may arrive at novelty. Here as in his metaphysical theories generally, there is a basic contrast —a contrast between the subject's initial objective world and his derivative, conceptual ideal developed through purpose. This transformation of physical by conceptual experience is given the name of appearance—an appearance, however, which must conform to reality to represent truthfully the inner meaning of both. The artist, we have seen, adapts appearance to reality with an end in view not only of truth but of beauty; and his result may bring the appearance more clearly into his consciousness than the former reality. Between the two there may be a symbolic correlation apparent in the function of language, music, and ritual, Whitehead notes, as well as in that of art.[23]

From reality, he says, springs the new occasion, attaining value in appearance that is "woven out of the old and the new."[24] Added to inheritance from the past there will be vividness of sense appeal and enhanced emotional feeling; there will be also simplification of the initial data through balanced judgment as the concrescence terminates in satisfaction. The process of unification, as we have seen, involves transcendence, a fusion of the ideal, the potential, with the real. Appearance then emerges into a new reality just as a novel occasion that perishes at birth remains in the world as value through objective immortality. The appearance of today becomes the reality of tomorrow.

An illustration of the lure for feeling effecting these results is suggested by Whitehead's own reference to Jesus of Nazareth as introducing a new social order into the world. Let us imagine Jesus with his disciples, his own peculiar world with which he has a special concern. As he looks into the hearts of his followers, finding there loyalty and devotion to their Lord and Master, and unselfish love, he envisages a greater beyond—the kingdom of heaven within the hearts of men upon earth. This is his lure for feeling, his eternal urge of desire. In the process of concrescence the reality of the simple faith of his followers is fused with the ideals revealed in his Beatitudes and in his thoughts of brotherhood and sacrifice—all uniting in a new goal for living. These ideals—mere appearance in the era when Christ lived—have indeed been realized during the history of Christian civilization, though obscured at times by disorder and evil. Only the fact that the kingdom of heaven has entered into the hearts of men could account for the good that has come into the world through individuals, institutions, and organizations. One might name at random Saint Augustine, Saint Francis, Martin Luther, and Albert Schweitzer to illustrate the embodiment of devotion, human brotherhood, unselfish love, and sacrifice. The service to mankind that has come through altruistic institutions and organizations needs no rehearsal. The humanitarian programs of the United Nations, however, arrest attention. In the medical assistance to under-developed countries, and in the promotion of their social and economic welfare through Point 4, God has been brought into the secular world.

The selfless character of Christ enters into Whitehead's concept of God as one who with "tender care that nothing be lost" suffers with his fellow creatures when disintegration of purpose hinders their creative advance. Though, according to Whitehead's interpretation, God has a di-polar nature, he is integrated as One, God in the world directing and sharing both animate and inanimate life. One side of his nature supplements the other. The basis of all order is revealed in the conceptual feeling of his primordial nature, which comes before all desire. Thus all subjective aim is derived from his primordial nature and includes in its lure a "sense of worth beyond itself."[25] In this way there is a prehension of each creature into God—the living expression of his other consequent nature, sharing the life of the world with his creatures, and evolving with the expansion of the universe. Being and becoming, the persuasive power of the lure and responsiveness to it through process as essential factors in all life, are thus in their permanence and fluency united. In *Adventures of Ideas,* the name *God* and the term *lure* have given place to the *Adventure of Unity* and to *Eros,* "the living urge towards all possibilities."[26] If Whitehead is avoiding the earlier terms as savoring of extreme monism or mysticism, there can be no denying that for him the creative advance of the universe depends on the participation of its creatures in a transcendence beyond mere mortality.

III

GOETHE, EMERSON, AND WHITEHEAD
ON GOD IN THE WORLD

It would appear to be purely accidental that late in life, Goethe and Whitehead used similar titles for their deepest thought in poetry and in philosophy on the miracle of creation. There is no evidence that Whitehead had any particular admiration for Goethe or for Emerson, who followed with fascination Goethe's studies in natural history. Like both, however, Whitehead, after giving concentrated study to problems of nature, was profoundly aware of the presence of God amid the actualities of this world. He summed up his conclusions in "God and the World," the final chapter of *Process and Reality*, as Goethe had done earlier in a series of lyrics under the general title of *"Gott und Welt."* Here are metaphysical ideas that in the form of maxims and reflections are scattered through his other works.

Ideas common to both Goethe and Emerson on the relation between God and nature, including man, would seem to foreshadow Whitehead's range of thought in the same area. Hence we would consider the views of Goethe and of Emerson in the light of principles underlying Whitehead's philosophy of organism and supporting his idea of the lure for feeling. In doing this no claim is made for Whitehead's indebtedness to Goethe or to Emerson. He seems to have had slight acquaintance with either one, for he was not in sympathy with the idealism associated with the early romanticism of Goethe or with the transcendentalism of Emerson. But Emerson gradually turned from extreme transcendentalism and subjectivity to a more objective view of man and nature, due in part, it would seem, to his constant interest in natural science, and spurred on by his reading of Goethe.

Emerson's attraction to Goethe, at first hesitant, grew by leaps and bounds as he followed with increasing fascination Goethe's ideas on natural philosophy.[1] Unfortunately readers of Emerson are generally more familiar with his disapproval of Goethe's aristocratic tastes, his love of a velvet life, pursuit of culture for its own sake, and apparent lack of deep moral purpose than with Emerson's enthusiasm for one whose "point of view [nevertheless] is always commanding."[2] Both Goethe and Emerson lived in eras when speculation on the history of the earth and of animate bodies was rife, continually changing and advancing. With views as opposed as those of Buffon and Linnaeus on a system of nature, and as those of Cuvier, St. Hilaire, and Lamarck on mutation of species, both were familiar. The authoritative statement of Helmholtz gives Goethe the credit of anticipating later scientific ideas. Evolutionary theories that were widely current before the publication of *Origin of Species* were of vital concern to Emerson. Such a common fund of interests was bound to increase Emerson's sympathetic reading of Goethe on natural history.

Studying German that he might know Goethe at first hand, Emerson, while still a young man, had browsed through most of the fifty-five volumes of Goethe's works, which were his proud possession. Plato, Emerson said, was the "eldest Goethe," finding connection and continuity everywhere.[3] "He must be a very strong or weak man," he wrote Covers Francis in 1837, "who can read his [Goethe's] works with impunity, without feeling their influence in all his speculations." After reading him for more than forty years "with an ever ascending regard,"[4] Emerson called Goethe a Titan whose "orbit is too large for common eyes."[5] Though more of a realist than Emerson, seeing life more objectively through his senses, Goethe as a thinker was yet in harmony with Emerson, who may have used him as a lens through which he read his own thoughts. The views they held in common throw light on later speculations of Whitehead, particularly on the place of God in his philosophy of organism. In various ways the views of Goethe and of Emerson on man in relation to nature and God, differed from the later ideas of Whitehead, but these differences were due in part to the time in which they lived. Evolution had not for them dislodged man from his central place in the universe. Yet Emerson's preoccupation with nature led him to see with Goethe how much man could learn from her processes. With the idea of creating like nature herself from within out, he was following, as did Goethe, the organic theory that stemmed from German idealism. But man's superior endowment of mind made it possible for him to build his own world. Whitehead gives emphasis rather to the mind's emerging from the world; but in the stages of process he sees a rhythmic swing from public fact to private experience and back again with a contribution of novelty from individual decision to publicity and value. Thus he expresses more definitely inter-relation and integration of man with his environment. To all three writers the impulse from within out may be of divine origin. Despite differences, awareness of God in the world and of His relations with his creatures was felt with equal distinctness by Goethe, Emerson, and Whitehead. Placing the views of Goethe and Emerson on natural philosophy, moreover, along side the more complicated ideas of Whitehead does help in clarifying his metaphysical theories.

One might select contemporaries of Goethe and of Emerson who, reflecting advanced thought of their own eras, also foreshadow scientific and metaphysical concepts of the twentieth century as represented by Whitehead. It would be difficult however to find two in successive generations so harmoniously akin, or two that in their common heritage as well as in their individual ideas are so linked with a modern philosopher and sage whose wisdom lies in his range of thought through nature's processes to higher phases of experience. The fact that from their respective backgrounds of thought three figures stand out to whom

Goethe, Emerson, and Whitehead were in various degrees indebted, is of further assistance. These three figures are Plato, Spinoza, and Leibnitz.

Our purpose in this study is obviously two-fold in attempting to point out resemblances in the work of Goethe and of Emerson on natural philosophy, and in turn their anticipation of Whitehead on this subject; but these two aims unite in showing a continuity of thought through three successive periods when scientific ideas were rapidly advancing. Goethe, Emerson, and Whitehead were alike in catching the spirit of their own times; in a sense all three were pivotal men, following the currents of contemporary thought, welcoming the new in their respective eras of transition, but not forgetting the old in classical tradition that still held. A continued interest in Neo-Platonism and Plotinus on the part of Goethe and of Emerson was one reason for their spiritual harmony; upon all three, however, Plato had a deep influence. From him, as has been indicated in Chapter II, came ideas on the relation between permanence and fluency, the one and the many, being, becoming, and perishing, and on the dominance of ideal forms, and the interconnection of all being.

The common interest of Goethe, Emerson, and Whitehead in Platonic tradition needs special emphasis with the recognition that in Whitehead Platonic influence is the most pronounced. The ideas of permanence and fluency or change, rooted in Plato, recur frequently in the poetry and prose of Goethe and of Emerson, and are basic in the philosophy of Whitehead. All three found inspiration in the *Timaeus;* among the later dialogues of Plato with which Emerson appears to be familiar, the *Timaeus* was his favorite, one to be read at early dawn ". . . as of a world just created and still becoming."[6] Here and in Plotinus he sees sources of Goethe's *"Welt Seele"* (World Soul): a permanent recipient of spirit from which life flows and to which, life, perishing in finite form, returns. In Goethe's thoughts that are Platonic or Neo-Platonic, Emerson finds a confirmation of his own. The theory of emanation, however, reflected in Goethe's *"Welt Seele"* and regarded more seri-

ously by Emerson, had no place in Whitehead's thinking.[7]
Discussion of the one and the many in Goethe's critique of
Moritz's "*Ueber die Bildende Nachahmung des Schönen*"
(On the Plastic Imitation of the Beautiful), in *Italienische
Reise* (Italian Journey), Emerson read early, reproducing
Moritz in his first book *Nature,* and making careful translations of passages that show the dependence of all particulars in nature on the universe as a whole.[8] The many
values of the evolving universe are for Whitehead incarnated in the One person of God as conceived in his consequent nature. The individual entity as one he sees also
arising out of conjunction with many. His notion of objective immortality germinated, he suggests, from his reading
in Plato's "Sophist" that not-being is a form of being. The
eternal value that Whitehead finds in objective immortality
Goethe sees enduring through perpetual change: "*Das
Ew'ge regt sich fort in allen*"[9] (The Eternal is ever stirring in
all); and Emerson observes in the world as "mind precipi-
tated."[10] It is the immanence of ideal forms in mind and
matter, in organic and inorganic life, that may have led
Whitehead to call the natural world the incarnation of
God. Perhaps for a similar reason it is to Goethe the living
garment of God, and to Emerson in early years the unconscious domain or memory of God. To Whitehead and to
Goethe the universals or ideal forms are actualized in the
world; to Emerson, in his book Nature, they retain in some
degree their Platonic character; but to all three they are
links between God and the world. As hints from Plato bear
fruit in Whitehead's own thought, summarized most completely in *Adventures of Ideas,* he sees clearly their effect
in the history of philosophy, which he sums up in good
faith as "footnotes to Plato."[11] Emerson in early youth
anticipated Whitehead's partiality for Plato in his question,
"What has reason done since Plato's day but rend and tear
his gorgeous fabric?"[12]

An essential part of Platonic tradition is mathematics, a
study of relations, we have seen, associated by the Greeks
with deity. It had not the same interest for Goethe and for
Emerson as for Whitehead, but the subject touched their

imagination. Although Goethe apparently distrusted mathematics in its application to physics, and, as Rudolph Magnus indicates, has been proved wrong,[13] he could hardly have expressed his keen admiration for Kepler and his discoveries in astronomy without recognizing the assistance given him by mathematics, his chosen profession. Goethe did indeed express wonder at life so immeasurably attained on this planet if nature in its lifeless beginnings were not basically geometrical.* Mathematical ideas Emerson pondered in his poems and essays; the geometrical foundation of the world is reflected in his poem "Uriel" and in his essay "Circles"; he finds no straight line in nature. He writes of the sea's "mathematic ebb and flow" and of "mensuration and numbers" in nature generally, as in the ellipse of the moon and the "balance of attraction and recoil" among the planets.[14] The importance of mathematics for Whitehead in the study of natural history, already noted in the preceding chapter, could hardly be exaggerated. It was a distinct aid in the shaping of a philosophy which he designates as a provisional realism. Both Goethe and Emerson like Whitehead later, find mathematical proportion identified with beauty; and all three, like the Greeks, see beauty and mathematics connected with law and necessity and thus related to their concept of deity. Not a mathematician like Whitehead, Emerson yet saw "relation and connection are not somewhere and sometimes, but everywhere and always."[15]

With this idea of the interconnection of all being, we have already seen Emerson associating Plato and Goethe. In making interfusion or inter-relatedness so important an issue in his theory of process, Whitehead refers to Plato's receptacle, the "foster mother of all becoming"; his ideas on God in the world, however, as well as those of Emerson and Goethe nay be made clearer by reference to later thinkers.

From Spinoza came the concept of God behind all ex-

---

* *Wäre die Natur in ihren leblosen Anfängen nicht so gründlich stereometrisch, wie wollte sie zuletzt zum unberechenbaren und unermesslichen Leben gelangen? Wilhelm Meisters Wanderjahre, XXI, XXII, XXIII. Aus Makariens Archiv.*

istence as a dynamic substance whose main attributes, extension and thought, might also be described as energy of matter and of mind. To his monism both Goethe and Emerson were attracted as Whitehead, we shall see, was not. But the relation of matter and mind we shall find of paramount significance to Whitehead as it was earlier to Goethe and to Emerson. Both Goethe and Emerson, who use mind and spirit synonymously, are indebted to Neo-Platonic influence in asserting that mind may control its own environment. Emerson goes to greater extremes than Goethe in his claim of spirit's dominance over matter. Yet, recognizing *natura naturans* as Spinoza's efficient cause quickening matter, and stirred by Goethe's theory of metamorphosis, Emerson sees that mind and Nature have their common source "in the life that rushes into us."[16] Although Whitehead finds mind emerging from nature and guided to decisions by the lure for feeling in process, it is yet the controlling element in the final satisfaction of a living occasion.

In Leibnitz the idea of organic development, greatly stressed later by Goethe and by Emerson, was beginning to emerge in the self-activity of his monads as they mirrored the universe and developed in proportion to their activity. The notion of Leibnitz that force is the dominating element of all life led to Herder's idea of energy throughout inorganic and organic nature—an idea evidently passed on to Goethe, whose relations with Herder as friend and admirer were familiar to Emerson. Both Emerson and Goethe were impressed by Leibnitz's theory of individualized monads and their driving force. Whitehead's basic doctrine of organic mechanism includes elements of thought from both Spinoza and Leibnitz. Like Spinoza, Whitehead recognizes nature's law and order in the efficient cause, but unlike Spinoza, sees God also as a final cause conditioning creativity, which for Whitehead takes the place of Spinoza's Substance. It is by introducing purpose through God as the lure for feeling that Whitehead bridges the gap between Spinoza's mechanism in the sense of adherence to nature's laws and Leibnitz's determinism through the pre-established harmony of God. Like Leibnitz Whitehead is a pluralist; his concept of living occasions is somewhat parallel to that of the former's monads; but the monads develop and change whereas the living occasions become and then perish. For Leibnitz, God is complete, the one perfect monad of his system; to Whitehead, God, though incomplete in his consequent nature, is eternal and the supreme example of an actual entity in the philosophy of organism.

Although Whitehead like Emerson earlier, finds science in relying mainly on the senses, more intent upon assembling apparent facts than getting at the complete truth, he makes scientific discoveries of major importance in the shaping of his philosophy of organism. It should be emphasized, however, that unlike Darwin in *Origin of Species,* he as well as Goethe and Emerson find purpose a determining factor in the evolution of the world. Developments in the late nineteenth and twentieth centuries, particularly in the fields of biology, chemistry, and physics, gave Whitehead knowledge and insight in his own investigations of nature far exceeding that of Goethe or of Emerson; but in their own time they followed closely the greatest contemporary men of science. Emerson was familiar with the work of Goethe's scientific associates: with Oken, for example, to whom he refers as a continuator of Schelling; and with Humboldt, whom he calls "an encyclopedia of science."[17] A knowledge of nature was as important to Goethe and to Emerson as it was later for Whitehead, in arriving at higher truth; and to all, the idea of purpose is linked with that of God in the world.

Science and poetry are as inter-related for Goethe and for Emerson as science and philosophy for Whitehead. Goethe's life-long study of natural philosophy is summed up in his *Weltanschauung* of "*Gott und Welt*"; and nature as the subject of Emerson's first published work, remains one of the absorbing interests of his life. It is a persistent theme in his poetry, and its influence may be seen in the development of his thought on metaphysics, spiritual laws, and ethics. It is the philosophy of being that arrests his attention as it does earlier that of Goethe. Of Whitehead's inquiries into the principles of natural knowledge, metaphysics was to be the climax, for his early nature studies led him to see the need of a system that should embrace all of nature including man. His purpose in constructing a body of ideas bringing "aesthetic, moral, and religious interests into relation with those concepts of the world which have their origin in natural science,"[18] is reminiscent of Goethe and of Emerson. Goethe in his novel *Wahlverwandschaften* (Elective Affinities) applies principles from chemistry to human relations, and he indicates elsewhere that we should turn to metaphysics for help in studying the problems of science. Emerson emphasizes this need in attempting to correlate nature with mind: "We have reformed our botany, our chemistry, our geology, our anatomy . . .," he writes, "but our metaphysics still awaits its author."[19]

The belief that science and God are not mutually exclusive, indeed that one may disclose the other, underlies Whitehead's whole philosophy of organism. The ideas of God in nature as felt through the eternal objects derived from him, and of God as a persuasive agent—a lure in process to beauty and value—postulate for him the presence of God in the world and in the heart of man, so clearly felt earlier by Goethe and by Emerson. Whitehead does not follow them in their receptiveness to pantheism; for him pantheism excludes the idea of God as transcendent. His belief, however, in a soul for every creature resembles that of Goethe and of the panpsychist Fechner. While taking his stand definitely on pluralism and a provisional realism that assumes continual organic development, Whitehead nevertheless leans toward monism and idealism, thus showing tendencies more pronounced in Goethe and in Emerson. Their monistic point of view was perhaps one logical consequence of early agreement with the idealism of romanticists; but their thinking also had a dualistic character that again foreshadows Whitehead. For them as for Whitehead the universe is dual because life within it shows both permanence and change. They also, like Whitehead, could conceive the world's immanence in God as truly as God's immanence in the world.

With the recognition of differences as well as similarities in the thought of Whitehead and these two predecessors, we may examine more closely in the light of Whitehead's metaphysical theories on God and the world including mankind, the early conclusions of Goethe and of Emerson that foreshadow concepts in Whitehead's speculative system. Within our given scope the impact of Goethe's mind upon Emerson may also be indicated as he read, marked, commented on, and translated passages from Goethe's works. On principles by no means new, but underlying Whitehead's philosophy of organism, particularly in connection with the lure for feeling, we shall compare the three writers as they add lustre to traditional and modern views of process, immanence, relatedness, interfusion, creativity, and transition. The order is dictated by the relation of these principles, which as a circle of ideas support and amplify each other. From process, in which Whitehead sees being "constituted by its becoming,"[20] one advances by means of immanence, relatedness, and interfusion to Whitehead's ultimate, creativity, and to the passage of events in transition. Creativity in its alliance with transition shapes the productivity of the evolving or expanding universe.

PROCESS

Process, we have seen, is basic in Whitehead's philosophy of organism. The organism is the occasion itself in process—a self-determining concrescence of entities. Goethe and Emerson were both concerned with organisms in their studies of natural history; and in their treatment of human activities, particularly of art, they reflect nature's processes, following the organic principle. The survival of the fittest organisms through natural selection is Darwin's major thesis in *Origin of Species;* Whitehead seems to be the first in the West to use the term in naming a philosophy. From the start of his metaphysical thinking he stresses in process "an underlying eternal energy" functioning in some sense like God by Whom creativity is conditioned.[21] In such conditioning God as lure for feeling guides the concrescence in process toward value. Reality in the becoming of any occasion, Whitehead indicates, is its emergence into value. Being then as the experiencing of value is actualized through becoming—a point of view held also by Bergson and James.

This emphasis on becoming is evident in Goethe as well as in Emerson; the thought pervades the lyrics of "*Gott und Welt*"; and in Emerson's journals for 1838 he says, "I am a becoming, so do I less sever or divide the One." In implying the divinity of man here, he is, however, neither with Goethe or Whitehead. According to all three, development is naturally organic—a passing on of innate qualities, and an acquiring of new ones as occasion demands them. Emerson sums up the method of nature in her assertion, "I grow." The subject, Whitehead emphasizes, through concrescent growth, reaches toward value beyond itself, and emerges as a new creature, to become a part of the world's objective immortality. Perishing to thus endure, it remains a lure to further reality. In calling nature the incarnation of a thought, Emerson is thinking along similar lines. A detached thought, he indicates in his second essay on nature, becomes in crystalized form a part of the world.

For both Goethe and Emerson God is an essential element in the becoming of the universe. Goethe's nature studies and his early enthusiasm for Spinoza result in the conviction expressed in his lyrics that God in nature moves the world. Emerson delights in observing "the Godhead in distribution"; in seeing "men that can come at their ends."[22] How they arrive at their goals, he says in "Experience," is by means of "vital force supplied from the Eternal." Here behind growth is power, a power akin to Whitehead's primordial nature of God, guiding the subjective aim through the various stages of process—the prehensions and feelings —and evoking an intensity that leads to final satisfaction.

As process may be initiated through the lure or magnetic attraction of eternal objects in the physical world, suggesting Whitehead's incarnation of God in his consequent na-

ture, we may use the sun to illustrate the lure symbolically as a source of inspiration. It was so seen by Plato and
so used by Goethe and by Emerson. The sun with *"dem
Reize des Lichts"* (the charm of light), as expressed in
"Metamorphose der Pflanzen" of *"Gott und Welt,"* is a lure
to the burgeoning of nature. If plants were conscious, Goethe
intimates in his maxims, to what wonderful perfection their
happiness in the sunlight would lead them. And Emerson,
carrying the same idea into human experience, would turn
". . . to the sun what we know is our best side."[23] To Emerson
the lure would seem to be instinct appearing in the lowest
forms of life and transformed in the highest types by enlarge-
ment to inspiration. By instinct the plant turns its leaves
toward the sun; in the glow of intense feeling come the
noblest strains of oratory. Emerson affirms that divine energy
in its intensity brings novelty into the world. The power and
value of this novelty, he dwells upon with such enthusiasm
as Whitehead shows more than a generation later.[24]

Organic development from inherited character to novelty or possible value in Whitehead's notion of process is
suggested in Goethe's discussion of metamorphosis, a subject of absorbing interest to Emerson. As early as 1834 and
at various times thereafter he referred in his journals to
Goethe's theory of the metamorphosis of plants, and marked
in Goethe's autobiography several passages on the subject.
Goethe's scheme or outline of metamorphosis Emerson could
hardly have missed, as it appears in the fiftieth volume of
Goethe's works—one that Emerson carried about in his
pocket and read at odd intervals.

Stoff

Vermögen
Kraft
Gewalt   *Leben*
Streben
Trieb

Form

Introducing this scheme, Goethe asserts that organic development can be understood only by grasping the idea of

metamorphosis.* In his two poems on this subject, the terms used in the chart appear: *Kraft* or energy asleep within plant or animal, and *Trieb* or germinating force that he notes in explaining his scheme must always have a support or guide. In the chart this support seems to be *Gewalt* or power synonymous with *Leben* or life. That this power is allied with God, whom Goethe associates with the laws of nature, is implied in the poems in his use of *die göttliche Hand,* the divine hand; *Gesetz,* law; and *Natur.* Metamorphosis then, applied here mainly to the natural world, is growth or becoming through activity made effective by divine power. *Vermögen* or potentiality, and *Kraft* or energy would seem to be quickened by divine power and by *Streben* or effort to *Trieb* or germination until there evolves a *Form* or pattern, which may suggest value as it appears in the philosophy of organism.

Emerson's notion of organic growth is probably best expressed in his essay "Experience." Normal growth he finds proceeding slowly. "That which is coexistent . . . as yet far from being conscious," he writes, "knows not its own tendency." But, he notes also, as evolution in the embryo is ". . . coactive from three or more points," forms or parts whose growth is coetaneous may ". . . one day be members and obey one will." Like Whitehead, Emerson notes the importance of the unconscious, but implies that in human experience the attainment of satisfaction or value through aid of the First Cause, though slow may be certain. Here "the ideal journeying always with us," like Whitehead's lure for feeling, may unify what is subjective and objective in experience; "insight," Emerson remarks later, "assimilates the thing seen."[25]

Unification in Whitehead's philosophy of organism comes through a growing together or concrescence. This is suggested in Goethe's discussion, in the *West-östlicher Divan,* of the poet's creative activity. Emerson made a partial trans-

---

* Under *Bildungstrieb,* creative principle.

lation* from his Cotta edition in Concord, indicating that the poet's pattern, material, and parts must fit together and penetrate each other in an aim toward value. *Wo Object und Subject sich berühren,"* Goethe had written in a letter to Schiller, *"da ist Leben."* [26] (Where object and subject touch each other, there is life.) There in the magnetic attraction of data that appeal as a unit to the subject of an occasion, Whitehead would say, is the driving power of creativity.

Emerson's ideas on power and form, though applied mainly to his analysis of the mind, find a correspondence in the laws of nature. From 1848, when he first lectured in England on "Powers and Laws of Thought," he gave nature increasing importance in its relation to mind and spirit. His idea of the mysterious unfolding of the mind like the growth of a plant, Sherman Paul notes, came probably from Goethe.[27] Such growth involves metamorphosis and specification, a problem Goethe credits to his Swiss friend, Ernst Meyer, whose words follow Goethe's scheme on metamorphosis, and so impressed Emerson that he made a careful notation:

The instinct of specification is the counterpoise of metamorphosis—the tough power of persistence of whatever comes to realization; a centripetal force which in its deepest grounds no outwardness can get the start of.

Metamorphose ist . . . der vis centrifuga und würde sich ins Unendliche verlieren, wäre ihr nicht ein Gegengewicht zugeben: ich meine den Specificationstrieb, das zähe Beharrlichkeitsvermögen dessen, was einmal zur Wirklichkeit gekommen, eine vis centripeta, welcher in ihrem tiefsten Grunde keine Aeusserlichkeit etwas anhaben kann.

---

*. . . *und hier wird Besonnenheit gefordert, dass Form, Stoff, und Gehalt sich zu einander schicken, sich in einander fügen, sich einander durch dringen. Werke VI,* 102.

This passage parallels Emerson's statement that "the daily history of the Intellect is this alternating of expansions and concentrations." Concentration, he calls the "secret of power"; and "expansions," he says, "are the invitations from heaven to try a larger sweep, a higher pitch than we have yet climbed, and to leave all our past for this enlarged scope."[28] Whitehead is not far from Emerson though less radical, when he brings the lure for feeling into process leading the organism or experience on to something new, and beyond the possibilities of what has been accomplished through the heredity and environment of the past. Power and form as expressed by Goethe make up for Emerson human experience, but an excess of either he deplores. Young men of great promise he sees often never acquitting their debt. A "sweet and sound proportion" may be kept only by acting in accordance with divine order, which Whitehead recognizes as limitation and conformity to what is good.

Like Goethe, but unlike Whitehead, Emerson identifies limitation and order with necessity, for which in *The Conduct of Life* he would build an altar. On necessity he had read and translated in 1836 a reflection of Goethe's in *Italienische Reise*:

Alles Willkürliche, Eingebildete fällt zusammen, da ist Notwendigkeit, da ist Gott.

Everything arbitrary, fanciful perishes, where there is necessity there is God.

Limitation Goethe sees, as does Whitehead, leading to perfection; but Whitehead in favor of free decision, avoids determinism. In *"Die Metamorphose der Thiere"* (The Metamorphosis of Animals) of *"Gott und Welt"* Goethe observes:

Diese Grenzen erweitert kein Gott, es ehrt die Natur sie: Denn nur als beschränkt war je das Vollkommene möglich.

No God widens these boundaries; them nature honors:
For but so limited may one hope for perfection.

Goethe is speaking of nature here, but much that he has
to say of metamorphosis Emerson carries over into his analysis of the mind. The quotation from Meyer on metamorphosis and specification Emerson must have recgnized as an
intimation of tenets in transcendentalism. The new democratic intensity in America was upheld by the transcendental movement. Men might be their true selves not only by
self-assertion but by self-transcendence; and the two theories need not show disharmony.[29] A knowledge of what may
seem beyond us Whitehead finds possible through the doctrine of significance, which, he agrees with Kant, "is an
essential element in concrete experience"; and he finds it
important too in recognizing the relation of "finite to infinite."[30] In connection with the theme of this study, it is
perhaps sufficient to say that the doctrine of significance
implies vision. To Whitehead as to Goethe, whom Emerson
quotes in his book *Nature*, "The wise man . . . in the one
thing he does rightly, he sees the likeness of all which is
done rightly."

Metamorphosis as organic development has special
meaning for Emerson in connection with purpose. "On organic action," he says in his essay "Courage" all strength
depends. Such action indicates to Emerson that man has
found his centre—what makes him really a man with a purpose in living. "*Das Zentrum findest du da drinnen*," (The
centre thou findest within) he must have read in Goethe's
lyric "*Vermächtnis*" (Legacy). Purpose or plan as an organizing principle, we have seen, enters into the philosophy
of organism; and in one of Goethe's maxims, which Emerson read with particular interest, attention is called to purposes in nature as well as in the works of man.[31] This emphasis was one of the reasons for Emerson's attraction to
Goethe. In an early sermon of 1830, Emerson insisted that
nothing is made without a plan.[32] Whitehead turns to radio-
activity in seeking a parallel to purpose as an organizing

principle, and finds purpose suggested in the diversion of energy in an electron. Is this then added evidence of a force behind a unifying plan of the universe? Herder in *Thoughts on History* had noted such a pervading dynamic force ranging from irritability in plants to nervous activity in man.[33] Goethe's praise of the book in *Italienische Reise*, Emerson was reading in 1836, and was sufficiently impressed to continue reading Herder and Leibnitz during the next two years. To them there must be a purpose, plan, or order in nature. How else to account for the reflection of the macrocosm as an organism and a microcosm in monads and the lowest forms in the universe?

Whitehead's organic theory has been recognized as resembling in some degree the monadology of Leibnitz, with the reservation that monads change whereas living occasions become and then perish. But what perishes, Whitehead adds, is not lost. Through its objective immortality, it will live in the future as causation.[34] By the actualization of transcendent aim in process the lure for feeling still remains and endures as magnetic attraction for other subjects. A thought allied with this idea appears in one of Goethe's maxims. *"Unser ganzes Kunststück besteht darin dass wir unsere Existenz aufgeben um zu existiren."*[35] (The whole device for us consists in this, that we give up our being in order to be. *Werke, XLIX, Aus Kunst und Altertum.*) The resolving of this paradox that perishing is the initiating of becoming he indicates in *"Eins und Alles* and in *Vermächtnis"* of *"Gott und Welt."*

Denn alles muss in Nichts zerfallen!
Wenn es im Seyn beharren will.

Into naught must all dissolve
If it in being will endure.

Kein Wesen kann zu Nichts zerfallen!
Das Ew'ge regt sich fort in allen
Am Seyn erhalte dich beglückt!

No creature can to naught dissolve
The eternal stirs itself in all
In life continue to find joy!

In Schelling's treatise on the World Soul, which greatly
impressed Goethe, is the idea behind these verses on everlastingness. The eternal element in anything, Schelling says,
lies in the fact that it is part of the Whole. Its being, of
however long or short duration, is preserved in the Whole
as everlasting.[36] The aesthetic values of nature, Whitehead
holds, "arise from the cumulation, in some sense, of the
brooding presence of the whole on to its various parts."[37]
Emerson sees man participating in this Whole of reality by
the presence of God within him. When the individual dies,
the universal element lives on.[38] The idea of perishing in
order to become Emerson implies in his own verses; in
"Woodnotes II,"

The rushing metamorphosis
Dissolving all that fixture is,

and in other lines from "Spiritual Laws,"

The living Heavens thy prayers respect,
. . .
Fears not undermining days,
Grows by decays,

Goethe would have understood with Emerson Whitehead's reference to the objectification of the world in God's
consequent nature. "The memorable moments in life," Emerson says, "we are in them, and not they . . . in us." He turns
to Goethe and *Faustus* to illustrate his meaning here. When
in later life Goethe was questioned by a youth on the meaning of a passage Goethe replied in substance: How should
I know? You are young, and can feel this experience better
than I.[39] The inspiration so far as Goethe was concerned
had died, but it lived on, in Whitehead's terminology, as a
lure for feeling. Every occasion, Whitehead holds, is pre-

hended into God in his consequent nature, having been guided to satisfaction by God in his primordial nature. The metaphysical dualism of Whitehead's thought may then be understood when he notes at the conclusion of *Process and Reality* "It is as true to say that God creates the World as that the World creates God. In both cases God is in the world: first as lure for feeling, guiding through his primordial nature in the various stages of process; then as an incarnation of the world, absorbing in his consequent nature all that becomes and has value. Thus is exemplified Whitehead's principle of process as 'being' constituted by its 'becoming.' "[40]

IMMANENCE

Process stops with the possible birth of novelty, which as value finds a place in objective immortality—the enduring natural world plus the contributions of man. All value is thus immanent in the consequent nature of God. "Where'er man looks springs the eternal" is one of Goethe's reflections in *Wilhelm Meisters Wanderjahre*, which Emerson read early in Carlyle's translation. The idea is confirmed in the first lyric of *"Gott und Welt."*

Ihm ziemt's die Welt im Innern zu bewegen
Natur in sich, sich in Natur zu hegen,

Him it beseems the world within to stir
Nature a part of Him, Himself in her.

The guidance of God from within we have seen in Goethe's interpretation of metamorphosis—a principle Emerson refers to again and again in his lectures and essays. "Convertibility we so admire in plants and animals . . ." he writes in his unpublished journals of the early sixties, "is the effort of God in the extremest frontier of his universe."[41] This observation calls to mind a statement in *Adventures of Ideas*. "Mankind," Whitehead writes, "is that factor in Nature which exhibits in its most intense form the plasticity of

Nature. "Plasticity," he goes on to say, "is the introduction of novel law,"[42] which he sees illustrated in evolutionary theories and derived in higher phases of experience from the immanence of God through the lure for feeling.

In the shaping of the philosophy of organism immanence is fundamental; here Whitehead goes back to Aristotle, who sees form actually immanent in matter as Plato did not. Whitehead refers to this fact in *Process and Reality* and also in *Adventures of Ideas*: first in noting Aristotle's protest against the separation of "a static spiritual world from a fluent world of superficial experience"; and next in observing Aristotle's theory regarding matter as insistent on "real communication."[43] To Aristotle matter could not exist without spirit—a thought echoed and positively asserted by Goethe. In *"Parabase,"* a short lyric introducing his poems on metamorphosis, Goethe seeks to discover *"Wie Natur im Schaffen lebt"* (How nature lives in creation)—the activation of God in nature as he creates; and it is the eternal One that is revealed again and again in all changing forms. Between the poems on the plant and animal kingdom comes *"Epirrhema,"* reversing the thought in *"Parabase"* of one in many to many in one—an open secret again true because of immanence throughout the changing forms of a single type. Emerson also sees immanence associated with the relation between matter and spirit—a question haunting him throughout his life. In the later passages of his unpublished journals, 'matter' and 'mind' or 'spirit' appear together frequently; he turns to Aristotle on the subject in 1849 for a definition of nature, and finally in 1856 he finds "the ground of everything immanent in that thing" and sees such a relation as organic.[44] This is a confirmation of Goethe's thought in *"Parabase."* Goethe's verses and Emerson's agreement also suggest Whitehead's doctrine of mutual immanence, in keeping with a philosophy basically concerned with interrelated organisms.

For the relation of immanence to the lure for feeling there is also a suggestion in Aristotle, since to him all things move toward God, the Final Cause, as by attraction to the object of desire. God, the initial 'object of desire' Whitehead refers to as he identifies God with the lure for feeling at the conclusion of *Process and Reality*. His own conviction that all appetition is drawn as by a magnet toward God, is moved by Him, is in line with Aristotle's thinking except for the fact that Aristotle does not make a distinction between unconscious conceptual feeling and thought.[45] Immanence in connection with the lure for feeling demands consideration of transcendence, which Whitehead distinguishes from immanence as Goethe and Emerson do not. His reason may be in part his rejection of pantheism, which to him excludes any idea of the transcendence of God. This limitation does not enter into the pantheistic views of Goethe and of Emerson. "God's immanence in the world in respect to his primordial nature," Whitehead says, "is an urge toward the future based upon an appetite in the present."[46] Thus he explains the subject's initial reception of the lure as appetition. The lure then in its transcendent phase becomes the subjective aim or final cause guiding the concrescence of the occasion to unity and satisfaction. In the process the lure as a persuasive power leads the subject toward the actualization of potentiality, which would make of it a new creature.

This persuasive power is not absent from the works of Goethe and of Emerson. God in the world is for them too a lure for feeling apart from technicalities. In the introductory poem of *"Gott und Welt,"* Goethe is speaking of spirit as intermediary when he says:

Es zieht dich an, es reisst dich heiter fort,

It draws thee on, it sends thee happy forth,

and Emerson's reference in "The Over Soul" to Jove rising above our trivialities and nodding to Jove over our shoulders implies a higher power that would lift man to his best self. "The receiver of Godhead," Emerson writes in "Experience," is led to ". . . entertain a hope and an insight that becomes the light of our life." The divine centre referred to by both Goethe and Emerson, and Emerson's emphasis on man as a spiritual channel convey the idea that God above is also God within. Highest Reason for Goethe and for Emerson seems to suggest Whitehead's lure for feeling. In Emerson's first book *Nature*, it is revealed as the stirring within us of higher powers. Before writing this book Emerson had meditated on the reason and the understanding from his reading of Coleridge; but passages in "Spirit" and in "Prospects" point to a quotation from Goethe's works which Emerson had marked in his own edition.

> *Die Vernunft ist auf das Werdende, der Verstand auf das Gewordene angewiesen; jene bekümmert sich nicht: wozu? dieser fragt nicht: woher?—Sie erfreut sich an entwickeln; er wünscht alles festzuhalten, damit er es nutzen könne. W. M. W., Kunst, Ethisches, Natur.*

> The reason is directed to what is becoming, the understanding to what has become; the former is not concerned with: whereto? the latter asks not: whence? She rejoices in development; he wishes to hold all fast that he may be able to use it.

The words *woher* and *wozu* in their English equivalents are three times echoed in Emerson's questions of the mind on matter. From Idealism there comes no satisfactory answer. With Kant and with Goethe, Emerson sees a distinction between reason and understanding, but, unlike Kant, sees no fixed gulf of separation. One need only feel with Goethe the miraculous in the common to recognize that throughout the world spirit is present. If man acts by understanding alone—"by penny wisdom," Emerson writes in "Prospects," he is exerting "but half his force." Through Reason the potential may become actual. "Nourished by unfailing fountains," he notes in "Spirit," "man realizes his infinitude."

The objective lure felt in the physical world—an indirect expression of God's presence—is seen in entities that have passed into objective immortality through the achievement of value in process. Their magnetic attraction is due to eternal objects that have been actualized in living occasions. Whitehead's objects have already been recognized as immanent; they are not copies of ideal forms. The beauty of a rose to him is a real beauty, not the shadow of something other worldly. Goethe had anticipated Whitehead by saying in *Wilhelm Meisters Wanderjahre* that the concrete or finite represents the universal not "*als Traum und Schatten, sondern als lebendig augenblickliche Offenbarung des Unerforschlichen.*" (as dream and shade but as living, momentary revelation of the unexplorable, *Werke*, XLIX). Emerson in "Idealism" of the book *Nature* reiterates Goethe's point of view, asserting that we may "behold unveiled the nature of Justice and Truth." In the essay "Michael Angelo" of the same period he insists ". . . that what is most real is most beautiful," supplementing this remark later as he translated from Goethe: "Who speaks not clearly to the sense speaks not clearly to the soul."[47] (*Wer zu den Sinnen nicht klar sprich, redet auch nicht rein zum Gemüth*, Werke, XXXVIII, *Einleitung in die Propyläen.*)

'Immanence' as used by Whitehead and by Goethe as well as by Emerson is concerned not only with the direct or indirect feeling of God's presence in the world. It is seen as heredity and environment, and may thus be associated with causality and purpose; it is also connected with aesthetic experience and with the order of nature.

Goethe and Emerson would both assent to Whitehead's interpretation of immanence as "the past energizing in the present." He felt the impact of both past and future in the present—"the whole amplitude of time." In *Vermächtnis* of "*Gott und Welt*" is a characteristic thought of Goethe's on the perpetuity of the past and foresight of the future that makes of the present moment eternity:

Dann ist Vergangenheit beständig,
Das Künftige voraus lebendig—
Der Augenblick ist Ewigkeit.

Then the past continuous in the present
The future glimpsed as living now
Make of the moment an eternity.

In "Self-Reliance" and in "Circles" Emerson finds "divine
wisdom" absorbing ". . . past and future into the present
hour," and life carrying ". . . in its bosom all the energies of
the past."

With this emphasis on the past as an important element
in the present, it is perhaps natural that Goethe and
Emerson should refer more often to efficient causation than
to the final cause. Both agree with Whitehead, however,
that God's presence in the world is allied with causation.
Goethe, impressed by his early reading of Spinoza, sees
God in nature as productive vitality—Spinoza's substance
or the efficient cause. The idea pervades his lyrics in *"Gott
und Welt."* Although these poems had not seemed significant to Emerson in his early reading of them, he later translated *Welt-Seele* in its entirety,[48] and marked two others in
the series. His reference to efficient nature as the quick
cause in his essay "The Method of Nature" of 1841, would
seem to be reflecting Spinoza, whom he had been seriously
reading, possibly in deference to Goethe's acknowledgment
of his debt.[49]

Whitehead, feeling that efficient causation had been
over-stressed in the 17th century, seeks to show its proper
relation to final causation. Heredity and environment he
sees as elements of the "immortal past" energizing in the
present; and in them recognizes the efficient cause. The
final cause he misses in Spinoza and is not satisfied with
what seems deterministic in the cosmology of Leibnitz.[50] A
subjective aim, which he associates with the final cause, he
feels is needed in his concept of process. This aim or purpose we have seen emerging from the lure for feeling and
uniting tradition or the immanence of the past with life or
novelty in the development of possibilities beyond the
present. Such novelty perpetually attending life, Emerson
had said earlier, is itself "a hint of endless being."[51]

In stressing the final cause, Whitehead is accentuating

the element of purpose which science and philosophy had been disregarding. But causality, Professor Hocking insists, "is compatible with purpose." Physical events, he says, lie in some causal series; mental events are in some purposive sequence.[52] This statement suggests a bifurcation of nature against which Whitehead protests; but is true in part of his occasions. Though physical and conceptual prehensions must be intertwined, he sees in the cause of each occasion its physical inheritance, and in its drive toward self-completion its mental reaction; thus there is a union of efficient and final causes.

Immanence in higher phases of living is particularly associated by Whitehead with aesthetic experience, as it was earlier by Goethe and by Emerson. Whitehead frequently refers to the achievement of art in finding unity through contrasts; a weighing and balancing to make apparently opposing elements compatible is a function of the subjective form or how of feeling in process. Concern for beauty is the outstanding how of feeling in aesthetic effort; and it is this concern that Whitehead sees linked with the foundations of the world and derived from the immanence of God. Goethe and Emerson see in aesthetic achievement the result of a divine impulse from within out. In accordance with the organic principle developed in the romantic period, both find art creating like nature herself. A familiar example is Emerson's linking of a Gothic arcade with a forest of great trees. It is the immanence of God, Goethe and Emerson never tire of reiterating, that awakens creative power. In the book *Nature* Emerson insists that man with his knowledge of ideals such as truth and justice "has access to the entire mind of the Creator, is himself creator in the finite." In the poem "*Wiederfinden*" of *West-östliche Divan*, which Emerson was reading in the forties, Goethe writes of two re-united lovers, feeling the anguish of their parting in the birth pangs of a newly created world. But the impact of the world's beauty brings a sense of power, and

Allah braucht nicht mehr zu schaffen
Wir erschaffen seine Welt

Allah need no more create
'Tis we who build his world

Self-creation and self-causation are an essential part of
process which Whitehead refers to repeatedly, but always
implying the background of God in the world. Man is
guided by the lure for feeling but must make his own decisions, which are responsible for the termination of the concrescence in all occasions. The more intense the subjective
aim, and it is God, Whitehead asserts, who evokes intensity,
the greater the value of the occasion or entity as it ends in a
unity of feelings that bring satisfaction.

God's immanence in the world, Whitehead believes,
accounts for a distinct order of nature in the universe. For
that reason pure chaos is impossible. Medieval recognition
of order in the natural world, Whitehead points out, was
generated in part by a belief in the rational nature of God;
and such a conviction, he insists, is essential to the progress of science. In *"Antepirrhema,"* which follows Goethe's
two poems on metamorphosis in *"Gott und Welt"* Goethe
gives a symbolic picture of the universe—the eternal
weaver's masterpiece of orderly and inter-related patterns
indicated in the metamorphosis of plant and animal life.[53]
"The key to all science," Emerson wrote in his journals of
1861, "is the unity of God." As Whitehead sees the order
of nature derived from the immanence of God, Emerson
finds man making himself a part of this divine order by
obeying his highest instincts as do the lower forms by their
structure.[54] In his last volume he repeats a thought from
Xenophon not unlike the principle already noted by Whitehead: "Without identity at base, chaos must be forever."

The transcendent appeal in the primordial nature of
Whitehead's God is foreshadowed in Emerson's "Oversoul"
and elsewhere throughout his essays; but to him as to
Goethe and to Whitehead, God is pre-eminently in the
world. "Here or nowhere," he insists in "The Sovereignty
of Ethics," one of his latest essays, "is the whole fact."[55]

RELATEDNESS

We have already quoted Emerson on relatedness or connection as being not "somewhere at some time but everywhere and always." In Goethe this idea of relatedness is equally stressed; it is fundamental in understanding Whitehead's treatment of creative factors in the philosophy of organism. All three feel the relation between the one and the many, between man and nature, spirit and matter, and finally between God and the world. "This notion of the essential relatedness of all things," Whitehead affirms in "Mathematics and the Good," "is the primary step in understanding how finite entities require the unbounded universe, and how the universe acquires meaning and value by reason of the activity of finitude."[56] He sees in the universe, as noted in Chapter II, two worlds that have a necessary connection: the World of Change or Activity, where living entities are becoming; and the World of Value or Persistence, where novelty that is also value endures. Either world would be useless without the other, for activity is meaningless without a purpose that can be judged; and judgment cannot be exercised in a vacuum. What becomes value later is earlier felt as potentiality—a possible ideal that is finally realized. Thus eternal objects are common elements in both worlds. The fusion of the two worlds, Whitehead also finds in the historic route of events or living occasions that make up personality and thus result in the unification of character. This idea we shall see suggested earlier by Emerson and by Goethe.

The traditional relation between the one and the many is illustrated in their association with the worlds of value and of change. The one is connected with value; the many, with activity and change. Thus the one may be the Deity in whom Whitehead sees incarnated the values arising from the creative advance of the universe; or the one may be the single novelty or value emerging from the world and arising from the conjunction of many. It is the former view that is emphasized by Goethe and by Emerson; but the latter view

Whitehead finds true by analogy. Both, he sees, are needed to understand how the world is constantly renewing itself. The stability of the universe requires the old, the many elements in a world already realized; but its creative advance is dependent on the plurality of values emerging from what has been and uniting with what will be.

As Goethe's deepest thought on this subject appears in his lyrics of *"Gott und Welt,"* Whitehead's supreme exemplification of the organic theory from the point of view of the one and the many, is indicated in the impressive contrast of God and the world concluding *Process and Reality*. The world as the unceasing activity of the many is intermediary between the two natures of God: his primordial, conceptual nature guiding process and thus infusing the One into many; and his consequent nature incarnating the objective immortality of the world and thus bringing the many together into One. The notion of the one and the many then allies immanence with relatedness, for as immanence through a universal element makes the many akin, so relatedness through mutual compatibility unites the many as one. To the Greeks the notion of the essential connectedness of things is associated with deity; and to Whitehead the concept of the "togetherness of things" is possible only through the doctrine of mutual immanence.

As a key to the unity of the natural world and mankind no principle is more enlightening than relatedness. Goethe and Emerson are, like Whitehead, assured that the purpose of God is the unity and harmony of the evolving universe; the term *evolving* having special significance for Whitehead. He expressed this conclusion after persistent analysis of elements in the becoming of the natural world including man. The same assurance came to Goethe and to Emerson through a different channel, through aesthetic appreciation of the beauty of the universe. All three find a degree of relatedness in the complete range of animate life. Relatedness in all parts of the universe was felt instinctively by Emerson as he began to write poetry; he understood then that the beauty of the world is realized in its composition—the whole design—rather than in its separate details. Such a

thought is basic in one of his early pieces, "Each and All,"
of 1834; he was to find it confirmed two years later in
Goethe's *Italienische Reise*, where Moritz is quoted on "The
Plastic Imitation of the Beautiful." This passage translated
by Emerson is echoed in his first book *Nature*.

> All particulars of beauty scattered up and down in
> Nature are only so far beautiful as they suggest more or
> less in themselves this entire circuit of the relations of
> the Whole.

> *Alles einzelne, hier und her in der Natur zerstreute
> Schöne, ist ja nur insofern schön, als sich dieser In-
> begriff aller Verhältnisse jenes grossen Ganzen mehr oder
> weniger darin offenbart.* Translation in Ms. 214.108,
> Houghton Library; also in *Works* XII, 217, 218.

In the poem "Each and All" Emerson also illustrates the
theory of the relatedness of all being—that "finite entities
require the unbounded universe." The charm of the spar-
row's song is lost apart from his native surroundings, and
the delicate beauty of the sea shells is apparent only

> . . . on the shore
> With the sun and the sand and the wild uproar

He sees too that according to this theory the universe loses
its meaning and value when its component elements are
torn asunder. Only when the underlying relationship between each and all in nature is secure can the poet find joy
in a world of harmony.

Emerson agrees with Goethe that the poet understands
best the relation between the various aspects of nature, and
marked in *Italienische Reise* Goethe's tribute to Homer's
knowledge of nature and to his skill in depicting it. Because of his better perception the poet "stands one step
nearer to things . . ." Emerson wrote in 1844. He is at one
with Goethe in his admiration for Hafiz, calls him the
prince of Persian poets and a mystic with a deep insight

into nature. His abandonment to the nature of things discloses their secrets and makes him capable of a new energy.
Emerson thus identifies with Hafiz the poet who

> . . . shared the life of the element,
> The tie of blood and home was rent:
> As if in him the welkin walked,
> The winds took flesh, the mountains talked,
> And he, the bard, a crystal soul
> Sphere and concentric with the whole.[57]

"Um die Natur zu erkennen musste er sie selbst sein"[58] (In
order to know nature, man had himself to become nature),
Goethe had asserted to a friend, and must have felt in the
wisdom of Hafiz the evidence of such knowledge.

Poetry for Goethe and for Emerson was closely related
to their study of nature, and Whitehead saw in the great
poets singular penetration into universal truth; but philosophy and science combined to absorb his attention as poetry
and science had for Goethe and for Emerson. Like the
Greeks, Whitehead approached metaphysics by first investigating the natural world, as in his *Concept of Nature* and
in his *Enquiry into the Principles of Natural Knowledge;*
and always a deep influence on his thinking was Darwin's
Origin of Species. To evolutionary theories Emerson was
plainly closer than was Goethe. The latter's interest in
natural history began early. His views on relatedness between the natural world and man must have resulted in
part from his acquaintance with Herder in Strassburg. Two
years later at the age of twenty-three, his ideas on the subject were stimulated by his reading of Spinoza, whose *Alles
Eins* he enthusiastically accepted. Some years were to pass
before he began his intensive study of botany, but it was to
Herder that Goethe wrote from Italy of his excitement over
the *Urpflanze,* his idea of the first original plant. Goethe's
record of this Emerson checked in his early reading of
Italienische Reise as well as his reference to the discovery of
the intermaxillary bone in man, an important link in comparative anatomy which became the subject of *"Metamor-*

phose der Thiere," in *"Gott und Welt."* The German scientist Helmholtz speaks of Goethe's studies in botany and comparative anatomy as foreshadowing future ideas in natural philosophy.[59]

Emerson's first insights into problems of nature came at the age of twenty, when he had shown some doubts and fears in choosing a profession, as he pondered with a growing interest in science the organization of animate life from mites and worms up to man. Some ten years later when viewing the many species of plant and animal life in the *Jardin de Plantes,* Paris, he expressed a deeper feeling of relatedness as an occult sympathy. And he said continually to himself, "I will be a naturalist." To the cankerworm, he noted in a lecture of 1836, the follower of Lamarck's system might say, "How dost thou, brother? Please God you shall yet be a philosopher!"

With such backgrounds Emerson and Goethe were naturally in agreement that to understand man one must study nature. Such a statement by Goethe, Emerson translated in his unpublished journals:

> In order to understand man; in order to unfold him out of the labyrinth of his structure a universal knowledge of organic nature is indispensable. Journal B (Part I) 1835-36.

> *Um ihn zu verstehen, um sich aus dem Labyrinthe seines Baues heraus zuwickeln, ist eine allgemeine Kenntnis der organischen Natur unerlässlich. Werke,* XXXVIII, *Einleitung in die Propyläen.*

In Whitehead's philosophy, organic life is explained by a complicated scheme for which there is no parallel either in Goethe or in Emerson. In certain broad general outlines, however, such as the classic view of the macrocosm and the microcosm, they were pursuing ideas to be developed later in greater detail by Whitehead. To all three, as to Plato, the world is an organism having a dynamic character and showing inter-relations; the many living things in the world, like the monads of Leibnitz, are also organisms mirroring in themselves the universe. Man and the macrocosm are clearly reflected in one of Goethe's maxims in volume 50, part of which Emerson quoted in translation in his book *Nature:*

> *Der Mensch kennt nur sich selbst, insofern er die Welt kennt, die er in sich und sich in ihr gewahr wird. Jeder neue Gegenstand wohl beschaut, schliesst ein neues Organ in uns auf.*

> Man knows himself only in so far as he knows the world, which he becomes aware of only as in himself and himself in her. Every new object well observed discloses a new organ in ourselves.

The thought that to know oneself man must study nature is an idea reiterated by Emerson from his first book until the series of lectures on "The Natural History of the Intellect" given as late as 1872. The reverse of this point of view Emerson also repeats with equal emphasis. Like a microcosm, he notes in the essay "Nature" of 1844, is the world man carries in his head; and again in his last series of lectures he finds our own organization "a perpetual key to the study of nature." In true Whiteheadian fashion, he remarks in an unpublished manuscript, "We say man in nature we may say as truly nature in man. . . ." We are interpreters of nature, he acclaims, "because we are made of it."[60]

References to man's body as a part of nature serve frequently to clarify Whitehead's theories on relatedness. He gives physical science the credit of establishing the principle that the human body may be explained by what is known of the physical universe, but insists also on the reverse of this principle—that the world may be interpreted by what is known of the human body. The body, he says, is composed of actual entities that may be so coordinated and inherited as to become an historic route of living occasions. This route endures as personality, reflecting in concentrated form the orderliness and satisfaction of social organization.[61]

Whitehead looks also behind life and notes the atom assuming the appearance of an organism with the inter-relations of its electrons, protons, and neutrons. In what resembles an organizing tendency exhibited in diversion of energy he finds something comparable to mental operations in human beings.[62] Knowledge of the atom in the time of Goethe or of Emerson was slight; but its mystery fascinated Emerson. His reference to genetical atoms of which plants and animals are composed, and his reiteration of the idea that all nature is in one atom indicate his advanced thought on the subject.[63] To find where life begins has motivated scientific experiments that have probed ever deeper into the nature of the atom. What has been discovered gives added evidence for belief in the unity of nature including man, and thus to relatedness in some degree between matter and mind.

Such a correspondence in the underlying laws of mind and matter both Goethe and Emerson emphasized in their time. Sir Humphrey Davy was making discoveries in electro-chemistry in 1807, which may have given Goethe an idea for his novel *Wahlverwandschaften* (Elective Affinities) started in 1808. Here the leading characters are mutually attracted through personal magnetism. Oersted's experiments in the field of magnetism continued by Faraday, led to Emerson's view of polarity in the mind as bias;[64] and he added to polarity as natural laws of the intellect, gravity, concentration and expansion, and detachment. Mind detaches facts actualized, he suggests, as the sun and stars throw off rings that may form a new planet. Little wonder that Sherman Paul calls him "the naturalist of the mind."[65] In his last lectures Emerson sees the analogy of the laws of nature and mind illustrated by chemical formulas, vegetable growth, and animal habits. Such relatedness Goethe expresses in lyric verse:

Getröst! Das Unvergängliche
Es ist das ewige Gesetz
Wonach die Ros' und Lilie blüht. Werke LXVII.

Be cheered! Life that endures
Reveals the eternal principle
Whereby the rose and lily bloom.

This question of relationship between the mind and nature absorbed Goethe and Emerson throughout their years
of writing; Swedenborg's views on correspondence between
mind and matter interested Goethe, and Emerson more
deeply, though he was not always in agreement. "Matter,"
Goethe says, "never exists without spirit, nor spirit without
matter."[66] (. . . *die Materie nie ohne Geist, der Geist nie
ohne Materie existirt . . . , Werke,* L, *Polarität.*) The interweaving of the physical and the conceptual in Whitehead's
theory of process shows a similar point of view. Mind and
matter, he insists, can not be torn apart; at least not in this
world.[67] Emerson suggested process in a living occasion
when he wrote in his journals of 1868, "We think by means
of matter." His ideas on the relationship between man and
matter changed somewhat as pantheism contributed to his
thinking. In his earliest work he finds mind dominating
matter, but nature's ministries are important, and while man
has fallen nature is still erect. As he goes on to speak of
man's command of nature through obedience to her laws,
of man's increase of power through sharing nature, and of
man's will as a counterpart of nature, he has less to say of
the mind's control of nature and more of the one animating power in both. "Who are we and what is nature," he
claims in "The Natural History of the Intellect," "have one
answer in the life that rushes into us."

A type of relationship very important to Goethe and
already mentioned in connection with Emerson, is *Polarität* (polarity). It was evidently derived from Schelling's
principle of identity in difference. The meeting of opposite
poles such as joy and sorrow; hope and fear; appearance
and disappearance as they work through each other, are
cited in Goethe's volume 50. Emerson was familiar with
the term in his early years from his reading of Coleridge;
and in "The Sphinx" carries the theory down to the atom,
which has its spheres of repulsion and attraction.

The journeying atoms
Primordial wholes
Firmly draw, firmly drive,
By their opposite poles.

On this question of relatedness in difference Whitehead is
definitely affirmative. In opposites, he insists in *Process and
Reality*, there is a contrast showing relationship; and the
recognition of similitude in dissimilitude he agrees with
Wordsworth to be a basic principle in artistic achievement,
for a sense of contrast gives intensity and value to experience. All elements as parts of a great whole also bear a
definite relation to each other. Whitehead's emphasis on
the aesthetic order of the world as derived from the immanence of God,[68] is in harmony with the thinking of Goethe
and of Emerson; their aesthetic experience, we have seen,
suggested relatedness in all being.

A relatedness in the historic route of occasions making
up the life of an individual, Whitehead finds particularly
significant, for the recurrent elements in these occasions
are the basis of personality. Emerson is in partial accordance with this thought in his essay "Fate" of 1860. "The
secret of the world," he says, "is the tie between person
and event. Person makes event, and event person." Despite
divergence from Whitehead in "person makes event," his
indwelling in the events of his life, which Emerson calls
the "print of his form," "fitting him like his skin, the chil-
dren of his body and mind," does suggest the recurrent elements in process which Whitehead calls the basis of individuality; but there is a closer parallel in the tie between
these events and the person with whom they are concerned,
resulting through their relatedness in the unification of his
character. In *Wilhelm Meisters Wanderjahre*, to which Emerson frequently refers, Goethe illustrates this point. He
recognizes in man the tendency toward the materialistic
or the spiritual in life. The interest of Montan in minerals
ties him to the earth and the more material things; the
absorption of Makaris in the stars lifts her to the heavenly
sphere generally associated with spirit. Although in per-

sonality there may be an emphasis on the spiritual or the physical, both aspects Goethe and Emerson see as Whitehead does later, are derived directly or indirectly from the source of all life in God.

To Whitehead, God's envisagement in his primordial nature of the total wealth of potentiality in the world, and God's incarnation in his consequent nature of all enduring values, combine as the final harmony of what transpires in the universe. Whitehead makes Him a companion of his fellow creatures, feeling their joys and their sorrows, and exerting "a tender care that nothing be lost." This may mean the overcoming of evil by good, for God sees possibility in each actual evil, which may be so transformed as to restore its potential good. Evil, on the other hand, as fragmentary purpose, may obstruct the aims of God as He seeks through the lure for feeling to guide toward order and the good. He remains, however, as the principle of concretion and limitation, and the One in everlasting Relatedness to the many in the world's creative advance.

INTERFUSION

'Fluency' is the term Whitehead uses to describe the concrescence of elements that are component parts of a living occasion. This internal becoming—the growing together of various elements that show mutual relatedness through similarity or contrast—might appropriately be called 'interfusion.' The idea of interfusion is a positive denial of the classic definition of substance accepted by Newton, as something sufficient unto itself. "No entity," Whitehead declares in *Religion in the Making*, ". . . requires nothing but itself in order to exist" and "nothing in nature," he had said earlier in *The Concept of Nature*," could be what it is except as an ingredient in nature as it is."[69] No flower, vegetable, or plant, one might add, would reach maturity except for its interrelation with soil, moisture, and sunshine. In connection with higher phases of experience Whitehead stresses a constant interaction of mind and nature. Mentality is not connected with space and time, he notes, in the same sense as are physical experiences; but it reacts to and integrates with physical experience, and from the interfusion of mental concepts with physical feelings living occasions arise. Their value is increased in proportion to the intensity of the feelings in process, which results in large part from the introduction of contrasts. Enjoyment of a sunset, for instance, we know is intensified when its colors show a striking contrast.

The epochal nature of time, which Whitehead ascribes to in his philosophy of organism also implies interfusion, and thus a specious present; for here the past, the present, and the subjective aim toward the future may be included in the duration of the concrescence. This epochal theory of time indicating periodicity or discontinuity of passage in contrast to the serial succession of time is allied by Whitehead with the idea of vibratory motion in the electromagnetic field. The electron's locomotion in its orbit may be represented by detached positions, a vibratory periodicity comparable to the re-enaction of feeling in the philosophy of organism from its efficient cause in the natural world to the subject of a concrescence. This re-enaction has a vector character in transferring what is there to what is here; and as with the addition of conceptual ideals a subjective aim and pattern begin to emerge, the reiteration of pattern during the different stages of feeling suggests to Whitehead the notion of vibratory existence.

Experiments and discoveries in the field of physics since Emerson's day have brought increased understanding of natural history; though Emerson was familiar with the work of Oersted, and heard Faraday lecture in London, modern analysis of molecules, atoms, and lesser particles would have brought him surprises as investigations of radioactivity since 1947 might have surprised Whitehead. As Emerson could draw inspiration from experiments in physics unknown to Goethe, Whitehead could make use of discoveries such as the quantum theory of which Emerson was ignorant. In his own time, however, Emerson had learned something of the structure of the atom from Dalton's atomic theory;[70] and he would have denied as emphatically as

Whitehead the idea of self-sufficiency in nature. "All forces are found in Nature united with that which they move": he observes in "The Sovereignty of Ethics," "heat is not separate, light is not massed aloof, nor electricity, nor gravity, but they are always in combination."

In Goethe's autobiography, *Dichtung und Wahrheit* (Poetry and Truth), there is an indication of the interfusion of time. A feeling very strong in Goethe, we learn, was that past and present are one: ". . . *eine Anschauung,*" he says, "*die etwas Gespenstermässiges in die Gegenwart brachte.*" (a reflection that brought something ghostlike into the present. *Werke*, XXVI.) This idea is implied in a tribute to the poet Hafiz, entitled "*Unbegränzt,*" in which interfusion is identified with organic unity.

> *Anfang und Ende immerfort dasselbe,*
> *Und was die Mitte bringt ist offenbar*
> *Das was zu Ende bleibt und anfangs war. Werke, V,*
> *Buch Hafis.*

> The first and last are evermore the same;
> The midmost then comes clearly bringing
> What stays at last and was in the beginning.

The same thought is expressed in the last stanza of "*Dauer im Wechsel,*" which Emerson marked in his set of volumes:

> *Lass den Anfang mit dem Ende*
> *Sich in Eins zusammenziehn:*

> Leave the end with the beginning
> To draw together into one.

Emerson sees the interfusion of time in present experience: "coming and past eternities," he says in "Woodnotes," meet in man; the Past, Present, and Future are, in "The Celestial Love," "triple blossoms from one root"; and in "Culture," man himself

> ... to his native centre fast
> Shall into Future fuse the past,

Akin also to the epochal theory of time are Emerson's references to periodicity in nature: in the solar system, and as a possible parallel, in the mind of man.[71]

In their concepts of the interfusion of nature and spirit, Goethe and Emerson both owed something to the Neo-Platonists.[72] After some concentrated study of botany, Goethe translated Plotinus from the Latin thus: *"Wie die Seele nur durch das Mittel des Leibes, so erkennen wir Gott nur, indem wir die Natur durchschauen."*[73] (As we know the soul only through the medium of the body, so we know God only as we look through Nature.) In his journals of 1855, Emerson quotes Plotinus on universal motion effected by the soul of the world. Here is suggested the idea of a concrescent universe—stars and planets inter-related in their apparent positions and various movements through the heavens. Disaster as the result of not sustaining the order of the whole, Plotinus compares to the fate of a tortoise in a great dance; because it cannot escape the order of the dance or arrange itself accordingly, it is trodden under foot. But regardless of non-conformity the inter-related movement of the spheres goes on; Emerson sees

> ... through man and woman and sea and star
> ... the dance of nature forward and far.[74]

Goethe stresses the interweaving of the relations of the great All with our being, and again and again denies the idea of self-sufficiency, as in *"Epirrhema"* of *"Gott und Welt."*

> *Kein Lebendiges ist Eins*
> *Immer ist's ein Vieles*

> Naught that lives is one alone
> Always it is many.

The interweaving of formative elements in the concrescence of a living occasion is basic in the philosophy of organism. In this connection we have seen the importance of eternal objects called by Whitehead the link between God and the world; for through them and the lure for feeling He acts as the principle of concretion. Envisaging the entire realm of ideal forms in their relevance to actual entities in the world, God aims, according to Whitehead, to achieve both order and novelty, which involve purpose, intensity, and satisfaction. The attainment of value must also mean a response on the part of His creatures to the persuasion of the lure for feeling. With such guidance Whitehead finds the self-enjoyment of one emerging from many to be the experiencing of value.

Science, he says, has found no such enjoyment or aim in nature because of its main reliance on perception through the senses. But Whitehead finds that continuity from the lower forms of life up to man reveals some persistence in basic feeling; for instance, in the instinct of self-preservation. As all life emanating from an immediate past anticipates through diversion of energy an immediate future, and occurrences from the lowest forms of life to the highest shade into each other, Whitehead sees in natural processes some approximation to aim or purpose. What of the flower, for instance, that turns toward the sun? Though purpose in human activity cannot be discerned through the senses, any lawyer, he says, is convinced of its motivating power. In man as well as in the natural world the immanence of the past energizes in the present, and the future as involved in purpose is also immanent in the present. It is thus in the intermingling of aim with other formative elements that the principle of concretion is evident throughout the animate world.[75]

The continuity of natural processes together with evidence of some principle of concretion points to God as the basis of order in this temporal world. In microscopic particles there is motion resembling that of the heavenly spheres. Within the atom an electron seems to whirl about a nucleus as a planet circles the sun. The key to an understanding of the cosmos, Whitehead tells us, is to identify "energetic activity considered in physics" with "emotional intensity entertained in life."[76] In either case there is diffusion or flow of energy. In lower forms of life he sees something of the intensity evoked in higher phases. Consider, for instance, a plant—the African violet when numerous blossoms are in bud. Examining closely, one feels a vibrant energy as taut stems seem to lift the large velvet leaves in the intensity of creation. All that is happening cannot be perceived through the senses. A perception of "the past settled world," a knowledge of atomic carriers of energy in the diffusion of moisture, nourishment, and sunlight, is needed to complete the picture of any *society* of living occasions such as the African violet plant in full blossom. In the various occurrences of life there is a togetherness of things. And their inter-relation or diffusion Whitehead has said requires a theory of mutual immanence.

This doctrine does not appear as a principle in the works of either Goethe or Emerson. The theory, however, is implied in the maxims of Goethe and in the lyrics of *"Gott und Welt"* as well as in the essays of Emerson. In Emerson's favorite volume of Goethe's works is this reflection:

> *Das Anerkennen eines Neben-Mit-und Ineinander-Seyne und Wirkens verwandter lebendiger Wesen, leitet uns bei jeder Betrachtung des Organismus und erleuchtet den Stufenweg vom Unvollkommenen zum Vollkommenen.*

> The recognition of a near- with- and into- one another being and activity of related creatures, guides us at every contemplation of the organism, and lights the stairway from imperfection to perfection.

Here is an idea of interfusion which points to Whitehead's more expansive view of concrescence in a living occasion. There is also a hint of this notion in *"Parabase"* and in *"Antepirrhema"* of *"Gott und Welt."* Eager to see how nature lives in the process of creation, the poet finds her

Immer wechselnd, fest sich haltend,
Nah und fern und fern und nah;
So gestaltend, umgestaltend—
Zum Erstaunen bin ich da.

Ever changing and enduring,
Near and far and far and near;
Thus a forming and transforming—
In amazement stand I here.

In the second poem he begs the reader to look with reverence at the world—the masterpiece of the eternal weaver
represented as the web or garment of God, and note

Wie ein Tritt tausend Fäden regt,

How one tread controls a thousand threads,

"*Antepirrhema*" possibly suggested the web of circum-
stance mentioned several times in Emerson's essays, though
the source for both Goethe and Emerson may have been
Plato's "Politicus," where *weaving* and *web* are used as
symbols throughout the discussion of society and kingship.
"A man," Emerson observes in "Uses of Great Men," first
given as a lecture in 1845, "is a centre for nature running
out threads of relation through everything fluid and solid,
material and elemental." Goethe notes how one tread controls a thousand threads of the masterpiece made by the
eternal weaver. And Emerson in "The Sovereignty of Ethics" adds to his earlier observation, "I am taught . . . that
what touches any thread in the vast web of being touches
me." In such emphasis on interrelation both Goethe and
Emerson are anticipating Whitehead's assertion that nothing
is sufficient unto itself.

Goethe's firm belief in the necessity of inter-connection
in phenomenal life, supported perhaps by his reading of
Spinoza, led to a warning in Volume 50 that students of
nature beware of isolated discoveries:

*In der lebendigen Natur geschieht nichts was nicht in
einer Verbindung mit dem Ganzen stehe.*

In the living nature nothing happens that does not stand
in a relation with the whole.

Like Goethe and like Whitehead in his constant protest
against the self-sufficiency of any entity, Emerson found no
life in isolation. "There is no solitary flower," he says in
"Powers and Laws of Thought" of his last lecture series, "no
solitary thought . . . To be isolated is to be sick, and so far
dead."

The interfusion in higher phases of life that comes about
through spiritual and intellectual experience interests Emerson. Poets are liberating Gods who give of their abundance
to others less gifted; and through our love for Shakespeare,
he may become our possession incorporated in our ". . . own
conscious domain."[77] This suggests a confession made by
Emerson about his own work that illustrates interfusion on
the intellectual side: "My best thoughts came from others,"
he wrote in his journals in 1855. "I heard in their words my
own meaning, but a deeper sense than they put on them,
and could well and best express myself in other people's
phrases but to finer purpose than they knew."[78]

For an understanding of interfusion as connected with
human experience and nature, Emerson looks to the insight
of the poet. "Rightly, poetry is organic," he tells us in
"Poetry and the Imagination," a lecture given in 1872. The
only way to know things is ". . . by taking a central position
in the universe and living in its forms," "We sink," he adds,
"to rise:—" From his reading of Goethe's letters to Herder
in *Italienische Reise* Emerson must have become familiar
with Goethe's methods of studying nature. Goethe's imagination as a poet was undoubtedly an aid in his discovery of
the *Urpflanze*. Interrelations he had observed in his botani-
cal studies as his attention was drawn to *"die Vor und
Rückschritte die zu gleicher Zeit geschehen."*[79] (the steps
forward and backward that occur at the same time, *Werke,*

L.) Goethe was certainly taking such a central place in nature as Emerson later recommended. *"Mein ganzes inneres Wirken,"* he writes among the maxims and reflections of Volume 49 with which Emerson was familiar, *"erwies sich als eine lebendige Heuristik, welche eine unbekannte geahnete Regel anerkennend, solche in der Aussenwelt zu finden und in die Aussenwelt einzuführen trachtet."* (My entire inner endeavor proved to be a vital incitement to discovery, which perceiving an unknown surmised principle, seeks to light upon it in the outer world and to establish it there. (*Aus Kunst und Altertum.*)

Swedenborg, Emerson compares with Shakespeare in poetic insight and notes that he saw the human body as ". . . strictly universal or an instrument through which the soul feeds and is fed by the whole of matter . . ." This statement illustrates partially Swedenborg's law of influx, which had appealed to Goethe as well.[80] Such identification with nature, according to Herder and Goethe and to Whitehead of the twentieth century, would seem to be not only a means of gaining scientific knowledge but of understanding intuitively the function of God in the world. From the world linked to God through the actualization of eternal objects, Whitehead says, the soul arises and endures. In the concrescence of a living occasion the soul is the subjective form or how of feeling; and in the self-enjoyment involved in attaining value, it grows in stature in proportion to its response to the lure for feeling.

As poet and naturalist Goethe found deep significance in his principle of *Polarität*—interfusion through the coming together of opposites. Feelings in human experience that show contrast, he indicates, may be united and through *Steigerung* (enhancement) ascend to a higher and nobler stage of feeling. In *Urworte Orphisch* (Orphic Words) of *"Gott und Welt,"* Hope rises from confinement and the opposing force of Necessity to higher altitudes:

*Aus Wolkendecke, Nebel, Regenschauer
Erhebt sie uns, mit ihr, durch sie beflügelt.*

She lifts us out of clouds and fog and showers
With herself; through her, wings are ours.

Emerson's two laws of Identity and Flowing or transition to
a higher platform[81] follow rather clearly Goethe's important
principles of *Polarität* and *Steigerung*. In his poetry Emerson illustrates identity, which he calls the science of wholes
and particulars—the basis of Goethe's *Polarität* as derived
from Schelling. Through contrasts Emerson sees in identity
an evocation of intensity; for example, in "The Sphinx,"

The fiend that man harries
    Is love of the best
and
    Lurks joy that is sweetest
    In stings of remorse

Experience for Whitehead has these same contrasting elements intensified and brought into balance by the subjective
aim as it emerges from the lure for feeling. *In Adventures of
Ideas* he suggests such intensity and balance. Civilized society may regard as the highest end a state of mind which
he calls peace. In attaining this end, beauty and tragedy
may play their part, bringing intensity of experience
through their contrast, but finally issuing into the balanced
intuition of harmony in peace.

"The event is what it is," Whitehead affirms in *Science
and the Modern World,* "by reason of the unification in
itself of a multiplicity of relationships." Such interfusion we
have seen to be apparent in all forms of life, and as a concrescence in process to be guided by the lure for feeling—
the eternal urge of desire. This guidance, according to
Whitehead, gives interfusion its importance in the creative
advance of the universe.

CREATIVITY

The principles supporting this creative advance all bear
a direct relation to the lure for feeling and thus imply a

mystic element in the philosophy of organism. This may be seen most distinctly in Whitehead's ultimate, creativity, which in producing value must always be conditioned or limited by God. Creativity's supreme task, Whitehead affirms, is achieved in terms of contrasted opposites: God and the World.[82] Contrasted opposites are also involved in Whitehead's principle of process—the constitution of being by its becoming; with God and the world, moreover, being and becoming are respectively allied. Process is in fact the method of creativity, which may be more clearly understood because we have already seen the relation to process of immanence, relatedness, and interfusion. Within the living occasion or process immanence plays its part as causation; and relatedness is a factor in the merging of the one and the many through interfusion. If such growth or becoming end in novelty and value, transition will be passing on what has become and perished to objective immortality. One can see why creativity in embracing all these phases may be called by Whitehead the ultimate—so important to him as an activity underlying all forms that he identifies it with Spinoza's Substance.

Indeed the eternal energy, in *Science and the Modern World*, underlying process suggests both creativity and God. In pure energy and productivity it anticipates creativity, but in its envisagement of eternal objects and possibilities of value it indicates the conditioning of creativity by God.[83] Later when creativity is designated as the principle of novelty, it is God in his consequent nature who judges whether novelty be value and worthy of objective immortality.

How creativity achieves its supreme task has already been adumbrated in earlier pages on process; but some larger aspects need further explanation. Generally speaking, Whitehead notes, creativity is protean in character, its creatures ever changing and growing into other phases of themselves.[84] Thus the universe advances as new ideas are entertained and new forms are created. Potentiality is actualized through response to the lure for feeling—the primordial nature of God that bears a part in all creative acts ending in value. And the part borne by the world in creativity or

growth may be described in terms of subject and object
structure of experience—an initial appeal of object to subject that results in the subject's appropriation of data. In
higher phases of experience Whitehead is particularly interested in what makes up individuality. With Plato's receptacle as the foster mother of what becomes, he compares
personal unity. Everything happening within it, he notes in
Adventures of Ideas, is conditioned by immanence, its own
past, and by transcendence, its potential future. The realization of past and present ideals in an historic route of
occasions establishes personal identity. These occasions he
calls in *Nature and Life* "unities of existence" in the creative advance of the universe; and the individual self he
describes in *Modes of Thought* as "that coordinated stream
of experience which is my thread of life or your thread of
life." God's part in creativity is felt largely through order,
limitation, and the evocation of intensity. Finally His fusion
with the world in the creative process leads to satisfaction
and value.

The protean character of a universe creating itself from a
divine centre, as emphasized by Whitehead, is an underlying theme in Goethe's poems of *"Gott und Welt."* Of
nature's perpetual activity and change in her creative
advance, he writes in *"Eins* und *Alles"*:

> *Es soll sich regen, schaffend handeln*
> *Erst sich gestalten, dann verwandeln;*
> *Nur scheinbar steht's Momente still.*

> Motion there must be, action creative
> First the forming, then the transforming;
> Rest there only seems to be.

In the unfolding of nature through the metamorphosis of
plants and animals Goethe shows particularly the protean
character of creativity:

> *Denke, wie mannigfach die, bald jene Gestalten,*
> *Still entfaltend Natur unsern Gefühlen geliehn!*

Think of what manifold forms now here and now there
Quiet nature unfolding bestows on our senses.

We have found Emerson deeply influenced by Goethe's ideas on metamorphosis. "And what seek I on any side," he notes in his unpublished journals of 1839, "but the transmigrations of Proteus?" And again between 1856 and 1859, "Nature forever strives at a better, a new degree." "The universe exists only in transits," he affirms in his last series of lectures, "or we behold it shooting the gulf from the past to the future." Much of his poetry reiterates the same thought. In "Pan" he writes of "Being's tide,"

But not the less the eternal wave rolls on
To animate new millions, and exhale
Races and planets, its enchanted foam.

This concept of the passing on of productivity, which is also an interpretation of transition, Whitehead asserts is basic in the meaning of creativity.

Creativity acquires its protean character through appropriation, which is what prehension really means to Whitehead when as a result of subjective concern the concrescent actuality would make the datum its own.[85] All phases of feeling in the philosophy of organism—positive prehensions, causal, conformal, and comparative feelings—are naturally concerned with the subject and object structure of experience, but contrary to Berkleian tradition, Whitehead would give to subjects and objects equal importance. All entities whether functioning as subjects or objects are alike in being potentials for becoming. In fact process shows the initial appeal coming from objects to subjects and these objects exerting attraction as a unit. To Whitehead such order is aesthetic order and such objects in conjunction "carry the creativity that drives the world.[86] Their feeling is re-enacted and reiterated in the subject until appropriation takes place. Thus Emerson's poet

Loved harebells nodding on a rock
and
A cabin hung with curling smoke

With Emerson and Goethe, however, appropriation
means rather more emphasis on subjective activity, especially in natural processes and in relations between man and
nature. Their common interest in the matter is seen in
Emerson's translation of a passage from Goethe's citation of
Moritz in *Italienische Reise:*

> Thence every higher Organization seizes, according to
> nature, what is subordinate & transfers it into its own
> being. Plants seize unorganized matter, through mere
> forming and growing. Animals plants, through becoming,
> growing, & enjoyment; 214.108, Houghton material.

> *Daher ergreift jede höhere Organisation, ihrer Natur*
> *nach die ihr untergeordnete und trägt sie in ihr Wesen*
> *über. Die Pflanze den unorganisierten Stoff durch blosses*
> *Werden und Wachsen; das Tier die Pflanzen durch*
> *Werden, Wachsen und Genuss;*

Man's accomplishments, Goethe insists, have come largely
through his appreciation and observation of nature. Whitehead would apparently be in agreement, for in *Adventures
of Ideas* he calls art the education of nature, and speaks of
it as "a fragment of nature." In *Italienische Reise* Goethe
writes of the effect of nature in Venetian painting, in time
measures, and in the obelisks of Egypt. These references to
the appropriation of nature by man impressed Emerson; he
marked several of such passages, and in his unpublished
journals for 1835 and 1836 noted nature's effects on man's
activities as seen by Goethe in Titian's painting and in
Egyptian obelisks. Through will power and energy of
thought, Emerson wrote in his book *Nature*, when he was
finding Goethe's ideas definitely exciting, man "takes up the
world into himself." Whitehead has a similar but less sub-

jective point of view in seeing man's mental life emerging
from his appropriation of the world.

Stress on individuality in connection with appropriation
is marked in Goethe and in Emerson as they deal with
higher phases of human experience. Goethe's own thread of
life or self-identity is seen in his absorbing of experience
before recording it. "What would remain to me," he asks, "if
this art of appropriation were derogatory to genius, . . . My
work is an aggregation of beings taken from the whole of
nature; it bears the name of Goethe."[87] This question Emerson copied in his journals with other extracts from Goethe
following his reading list for 1834; the relation of appropriation to organic development in human experience as well as
in nature was evidently important to him.[88] In his essay
"Experience," subjectiveness is emphasized by its alliance
with appropriation. "All I know," he writes, "is reception; I
am and I have. . . ." And again: "The subject exists, the
subject enlarges; all things sooner or later fall into place."

In seeing the necessity for order and limitation in the
aesthetic process Goethe and Emerson come close to Whitehead. Their emphasis is on the laws of art; and Whitehead
claims that the aesthetic order, based on the ideals of unity
and harmony, is derived from the immanence of God. Value
in process is largely dependent upon God's participation as
the ground of concretion and the principle of limitation.
This is His part in the task of creativity to be achieved in
the terms of contrasting opposites: God and the World.
How this is possible, Whitehead explains by turning to
artistic creation. It is the aesthetic urge, he says in *Religion
in the Making*, that is basic in the creative process. The
impulse that starts the action is an "uprush of feeling" or
yearning for satisfaction awakening a sense of power in relation to concrete activity.[89] As in higher phases of experience
the lure develops a subjective aim embracing order and
purpose, it must also suggest limitation, a weighing and
balancing of the elements that enter into concrescence or
growth. Free creation, Goethe insisted earlier, is made possible by limitation, a law or measure which Whitehead,
familiar with Plato's class of the limit in the *Philebus*, iden-

tifies with God as conditioning activity. In the productive processes of nature Goethe finds limitation an organic necessity. In lines on nature and art, he applies this law to human achievement:

> *Wer grosses will muss sich zusammen raffen:*
> *In der Beschränkung zeigt sich erst der Meister*
> *Und das Gesetz nur kann uns Freiheit geben.*
> *(Natur und Kunst)*, XLVII.

> Who greatness wishes must collect himself
> Mastery in restraint does first appear
> And to us law alone can freedom give.

These lines are paralleled in Emerson's message of the spirits to the poet:

> Brother, sweeter is the Law
> Than all the grace Love ever saw;
> We are its suppliants. By it, we
> Draw the breath of Eternity;

The recognition of the function of limitation for the lure qualifies Whitehead's notion of a self-creating universe. Man, though guided by the lure, is free to make his choice. Nature is free, Goethe indicates, through blind necessity; man, Emerson adds, through voluntary obedience. To Whitehead novelty or value is achieved only when God enters into the process of creation. Satisfactory results come through His evocation of intensity. Emerson's assertion that potentiality is realized by "vital force supplied by the eternal" suggests the intensity that brings about the final satisfaction of Whitehead's living occasion. Goethe had expressed the idea of satisfaction in creative achievement somewhat differently in "*Vermächtnis*" of "*Gott und Welt.*"

> *Und war es endlich dir gelungen,*
> *Und bist du vom Gefühl durchdrungen:*
> *Was fruchtbar ist, allein ist wahr.*

And then at last success achieved
And yearning satisfied indeed
What fruitful is, alone is true.

To Goethe *"Gefühl ist alles,"* Emerson would make himself a pure and "permeable channel" for Heaven to flow to
earth, and thus the "fulness of its reception" [his feeling]
would make for the truth and wholeness of his ultimate aim
—his fruits of the spirit. By making himself a channel, he
said in his last series of lectures, he may also preserve his
personal identity and recognize the ". . . one thread, fine as
gossamer and yet real," which is his own thread of life,
". . . the thread on which for him the earth and the heaven
of heavens are strung."[90a] This would indeed mean intensity
of experience and depth of satisfaction, with which Whitehead feels God is more concerned than with aught else in
the achievement of his purposes.[90b]

The value of creativity for Whitehead is seen when a
process ends in objective immortality, for this points to the
fusion of God and the world. Such a fusion of the ideal and
the actual Goethe shows in his comparison of creative
power and nature: ". . . *die Bildungskraft . . . erzeugt, wie
die Natur, den Abdruck ihres Wesen aus sich selber.*" This
statement, which reflects the German organic principle,
Emerson read in *Italienische Reise* and translated thus:
"Creative power stamps like nature the impression of its
being out of itself."[91] In the artist as in nature, Goethe indicates, creativity works out to the world from a divine
centre. It was the inner vision of Phidias, Goethe translated
from Plotinus, that enabled him to create an image of Zeus.

*So konnte Phidias den Gott bilden, ob er gleich nichts
sinnlich Erblickliches nachahmte, sondern sich einen
solchen in dem Sinn fasste wie Zeus selbst erscheinen
würde, wenn er unsern Augen begegnen möchte.*

And Emerson in turn translating Goethe from his letters to
Zelter, wrote in his journal for 1837:

So could Phidias form the God, although he imitated
nothing perceptible to the senses, but made himself, in
his mind, such a form as Jove himself would appear if
he should become obvious to our eyes.

As Emerson's poem, "The Problem" was also composed in
the year 1837, the impact of Goethe's mind through his ren-
dering of Plotinus seems evident in Emerson's references
here to art:

Not from a vain or shallow thought
His awful Jove young Phidias wrought

The sculptor's creative power was rather a realization of his
own inspired vision. Emerson's lines in the same poem on
Michelangelo's creation of St. Peter's show the genius of
the architect working from within out; and they anticipate
Whitehead's theory that creative action is conditioned by the
fusion of the actual and the transcendent ideal.

Himself from God he could not free
He builded better than he knew
The conscious stone to beauty grew.

It is thus in artistic creativity, particularly in poetry, that
Emerson like Goethe finds the fusion of the concrete and the
ideal exemplified. In Shakespeare as in nature he sees the
formative elements of creation lying in the intermixture of
the common and the transcendental. In his maxims Goethe
calls attention to such intermingling of the *Besondere*
(particular) with the *Allgemeine* (universal) or Plato's
ideals. To Goethe the presence of the universal in the particular may result in an immediate, living revelation of the
divine. Emerson, recurring frequently to the idea of the
miraculous in the common, says in his last series of lectures,
"I owe to genius always the great debt of lifting the curtain
from the common and showing me that gods are sitting dis-
guised in every company."

The magnetic attraction of the universal in the particular is an illustration of Whitehead's eternal objects as they function in the objective immortality of the world, and in its expanding creative advance; they are thus links between God and the world. The objective lure leads from the entities in which immanence has already been realized, as does the subjective lure from derivative guidance, to an urge toward potential action. The mountain peak rising up before Wordsworth in his childhood and prompting him to return a stolen boat, symbolized to him the "Wisdom and Spirit of the universe." Whitehead in his blending of the immanent and the transcendent as the means of conditioning creativity, is in agreement with the meaning of immanence as interpreted by Goethe and by Emerson. Goethe sees the deity within the world acting upon it in its process of becoming:

Ihm ziemt's die Welt im Innern zu bewegen
. . .
So das, was in ihm lebt und webt und ist,
Nie seine Kraft, nie seinen Geist vermisst.
"Proemium" of "Gott und Welt."

He seems the world within to stir
. . .
So that what in Him lives and moves and is
Can ne'er his strength nor e'er his spirit miss.

And Emerson adds a moral note as divine persuasion—the eternal urge—stirs a responsive chord in youth to creative action:

So nigh is grandeur to our dust,
So near is God to man,
When Duty whispers low, *Thou must,*
The youth replies, *I can.* "Voluntaries," III.

To Whitehead, "the things which are temporal arise by their participation in the things which are eternal"; Emerson

in his time conceives the true order of nature, in accordance
with Plato, as the visible ". . . proceeding from the invisible . . .";[92] and on the same hypothesis Goethe still earlier
bases his whole philosophy of nature.

So weit das Ohr, so weit das Auge reicht,
Du findest nur Bekanntes, das ihm [Gott] gleicht,

So far as ear, so far as eye can reach
All that is known is found like unto Him,

TRANSITION

Transition is so closely allied with creativity in the progress of the universe that Whitehead finds the meaning of
productivity and carrying on in both. This close connection
one may be helped to understand by considering what the
subject or *subject-superject* means to Whitehead in comparison with the *superject*. The fluency of concrescence is one
meaning Whitehead gives to transition. Over the fluency of
its own immediacy the subject presides in private enjoyment, aiming as subject toward the satisfaction of subject
superject. With value achieved the subject perishes; and
only the superject remains in objective immortality, in the
world from which its components came. The superject then
is a public matter of fact and is designated by Whitehead
as "a moment of passage from decided public facts to a
novel public fact." Such a transition means more than a mere
linear progression. The passage of things, he insists, is "one
all-pervasive fact"[93] involving time and space. It could not
be otherwise to one who affirms reality as process. But the
living occasion, the unit of process, Whitehead says, does
not move; by means of changing internal relations it only
becomes. The fluency of a concrescence, however, through
which an entity becomes, is also termed by Whitehead
transition—a flowing that suggests, according to Plato, imperfection or limitation of something that is not what it
might be. Such motion Whitehead had seen in Plato, as had
Goethe and Emerson earlier, is initiated by the soul: the

soul in the *Timaeus* making a cosmos out of chaos; and Psyche in the *Symposium* acting as a persuasive power on Eros in the ascent toward beauty. Change or transition from privacy to publicity and back again is Whitehead's more frequent use of the term. Where a passage of events may lead, he notes in his early work on nature, is "beyond our ken"; and in the metaphysical scheme of *Process and Reality,* he indicates that the primordial nature of God envisages the relevance of the past to present and future potentiality as man cannot, and through His persuasive power the progress of the world is determined.

Spinoza as well as Plato is reflected in Whitehead's view of transition, and also in that of the two earlier writers, Goethe and Emerson. The process of transition in gathering up the past and passing on the efficient cause, Whitehead sees functioning like Spinoza's substance. But this flux of energy, which to Emerson and to Goethe is in the main continuous, would for Whitehead, in accordance with later scientific theories, show discontinuity. The vibratory locomotion of an electron in its orbit within the atom in a series of detached positions, and its vibratory deformation as it changes its pattern, suggest to him the concept, already mentioned, of vibratory existence. Such vibration or reiteration he sees in his living occasions during various stages of feeling as their pattern is reproduced, but not "with undifferentiated sameness." Feeling emanating from the physical world is intensified in the subject by conceptual objects derived from this initial feeling; then periodic decisions that accompany the merging of the inherited past or efficient cause with transcendent aims may bring satisfaction and a return to the material world. Thus in this rhythmic character of vibration Whitehead sees constant renewal and unification of the world. The theory of vibration would arrest continuity, but would add intensity to what Whitehead affirms of immanence and relatedness in all life. A combination of these three principles has been called essential in the structure of his organic philosophy.[94]

With less scientific knowledge, both Goethe and Emerson find in the rhythmical pulsation of nature certain exceptions to the continuity of transition; as in contraction and expansion and in motion and rest. And in line with Swedenborg's law of correspondence they carry over rhythmical changes into human experience. Man must first collect himself if he would succeed, according to Goethe; must concentrate if he would expand, according to Emerson. Both find highest reason, like Whitehead's lure, pointing to potentiality; transcendence then as conceived by Whitehead merges with immanence in all three as value is achieved.

In proclaiming metamorphosis Goethe and Emerson recognize that transition is the one all pervasive fact in nature; but while they hold to the classical idea of circular motion, Whitehead's thought in all phases of his metaphysical system, is rooted in the modern theory of relativity. That there is a rhythmical flow of life as the universe renews itself, we have seen in Whitehead's theory of creativity: its initiation from the physical world and its passing back into objective immortality. Hence he would agree in part with observations made by Goethe and by Emerson on the subject of transition. Goethe upholds early the circular path of nature's dance, so termed by Plotinus. Nature has no notion of standing still, and has reserved such freedom for herself that with the help of knowledge and science she can hardly be reached or driven into a corner. Emerson begins in "The American Scholar" to note the inexplicable continuity in nature ". . . always circular power returning into itself." "We can never surprise nature in a corner,"[95] he says in "The Method of Nature," echoing Goethe. That all things are flowing, even those that seem immovable, he indicates in undated verses entitled "Transition."

> See yonder leafless trees against the sky,
> How they diffuse themselves into the air,
> And ever-subdividing, separate
> Limbs into branches, branches into twigs,
> As if they loved the elements, and hasted
> To dissipate their being into it.

Goethe sees the power of revolving action as the highest gift of God and nature to man. Its inspiration comes from the soul as had the life of the world in Plato's *Timaeus*, source of *"Weltseele,"* the first poem written by Goethe in the series of *"Gott und Welt."* The animating power that in the *Timaeus* moves the universe, and in this sense suggests Whitehead's lure for feeling, Goethe calls upon in *"Eins und Alles"* to penetrate his being that he may progress to his highest capacity:

> *Weltseele, komm uns zu durchdringen!*
> *Dann mit dem Weltgeist selbst zu ringen,*
> *Wird unsrer Kräfte Hochberuf.*

> Soul of the World, come pierce us through
> Then with thy help our work to do
> May come the challenge to our powers.

To the lure Whitehead looks for a similar quickening of the spirit. The idea of transition as flowing from the imperfect to what might be underlies Emerson's allusions to method in art and poetry. He finds the sculptor representing a hero or god by turning from what is perceptible to the senses, to the ideal world that is not so perceived.[96] It is the poet or inventor, Emerson says, who knows best how to use the past in reaching toward new life or novelty; he it is who "unlocks our chains," who "admits us to a new scene." "Creation," Emerson insists in his lecture on "Poetry and the Imagination," in 1872, "is always on wheels in transit, always passing into something higher." "By reason of transition," Whitehead says in *Process and Reality*, "the actual world is always a relative term." He might have echoed Plato with the words, "It never really is."

Goethe in one of the maxims in Emerson's favorite volume, asserts that Nature is life and consequences flowing out from an unknown centre to boundaries that we cannot discern. And this indeed has seemed to be the course of evolution. Passage as the one all-pervasive fact Whitehead had seen involved change from one form to another accord-

ing to Darwin's *Origin of Species*. Goethe pointed toward
such changes in his discovery of the intermaxillary bone,
and in his *"Metamorphose der Thiere"* in *"Gott und Welt."*
Emerson, living in the period immediately preceding Darwin's book, saw more clearly than Goethe the implications
of evolution; as in "Woodnotes,"

> . . . the eternal Pan
> Who layeth the world's incessant plan,
> Halteth never in one shape,
> But forever doth escape,
> Like wave or flame, into new forms
> Of gem and air, of plants, and worms.

Transition is miraculous, Emerson says, in that we see no
more the end than the beginning; and the miracle of this
transit, he names in his journals for 1841 as God—to Whitehead the ground of all concretion. The poet, better than
another, Emerson finds, has insight into this process and
change. His most familiar lines on this theme come again
from "Woodnotes II":

> Sweet the genesis of things
> Of tendency through endless ages,
> Of star-dust, and star-pilgrimages,
> Of rounded worlds, of space and time,

And man emerging from nature at large is moving toward
development we can merely conjecture,

> Horsed on the Proteus
> Thou ridest to power
> And endurance.[97]

To Goethe the constant striving toward something higher
is the secret of achievement; this idea is illustrated not only
in the continued zest of Faust for nobler enterprise in Part
II of the drama, but also in Goethe's own life. Emerson
takes up the thought with his emphasis on transition in his

last journal as "the organic destiny of the mind"—"ever the
ascending effort"—and calls attention to the ascending scale
of Plato in "The Symposium." The health of the mind, he
notes, is seen as it passes "by deceptive leaps forward into
new states."[98] "Power ceases," he had observed in "Self-
Reliance," "in the instant of repose." In the last entries of
Emerson's journals transition is a recurrent topic. As he saw
the organic destiny of the mind in transition, he could say
of human development as of nature's processes, ". . . the
more transit, the more continuity; . . . [but of man alone]
we are immortal by force of transits."[99]

Such transits, to Whitehead, are marked from occasion
to occasion in the historic route of human experience that
mirrors personal identity. The evocation of intensity in
living occasions may mean, according to him, a gradual
recognition of value through the potency of the lure for
feeling. Step by step decisions that may lead to satisfaction
are carefully weighed before the completion of an event
worthy of transition to objective immortality. In Whitehead's philosophy the idea of immortality does not go beyond this world. But wherever identity may endure or
immortality be established, it is clear from the thought of
Goethe, Emerson, and Whitehead that with guidance from
the lure of God in the world, man himself is a large factor
in the determination of his immortality. We are, as Emerson
declares, "immortal by force of transits."

Thus we come to the end of a tentative approach to
Whitehead through two outstanding men of letters. Principles which we have found underlying the philosophy of
organism, form a circle amplifying each other and reiterated
from various angles, but centred in the lure for feeling or
the presence of God in the world. That was Whitehead's
angle of vision—his adventure of the spirit as he sought to
account for the production of novelty and value in the creative advance of the universe. Anticipated in some degree by
Goethe and by Emerson, he penetrates more deeply than
they into the mystery of being. Neither Goethe nor Emerson would claim any technical knowledge of metaphysics;
yet both show a metaphysical point of view in their treat-

ment of natural history and in their focus on the relatedness of nature, man, and God.

The results of Emerson's reading of Goethe have been confined to the framework we have set up; but within this scope, the number of passages that Emerson marked or translated, the comments he made, the ideas parallel to those of Goethe as well as the echoes of Goethe's phrases in his own works, indicate a deeper interest of Emerson in Goethe than has yet perhaps been realized.

Belief in a rational order of nature as indicative of God in the world is for them as for Whitehead essential to the progress of science. But the converging of the thought of all three in respect to the lure for feeling may be seen at best in their common sharing in the spirit of the mystic as well as in the objective attitude of the realist. That the true mystic must also be a realist, Professor Hocking has emphasized in his latest book, *The Meaning of Immortality in Human Experience.*[100] Life, he says, has meaning to the mystic in proportion to his growth—a meaning in that he feels himself constantly led toward a possible fulfillment; and thus he is in alliance with purpose and God.[101] In reading the work of Goethe or of Emerson, one could not miss this attitude; and it must have entered largely into Whitehead's thinking as he developed his idea of the lure for feeling in the philosophy of organism.

IV

BURROUGHS AND WHITMAN—
NATURALIST AND MYSTIC

The following of John Burroughs in America during the last four decades of his life, Norman Foerster points to as tremendous.[1] Yet Burroughs may come to be remembered best as comrade of Whitman from early acquaintance in 1863 until the poet's death.[2] Possibly the most understanding of Whitman's early biographers and critics, Burroughs had eyes to see that the author of *Leaves of Grass* was in the great world current. One stream of this current that had carried on Goethe and Emerson as well, Whitehead was to name the rise of naturalism, coming before the rise of science.[3] Since Burroughs' own intimate knowledge of nature led to his wide reading of science, he could understand Goethe's delight in exploring the natural world and his resultant scientific bent. Quotations from this area of Goethe's thought, in translation, are scattered through Burroughs' works. To Emerson's observations on natural history he gives more attention, knowing it was Emerson who helped Whitman to find himself. Since Goethe and Emerson are both quoted by Burroughs on principles which he pondered, and which we have already seen underlying the philosophy of organism, some further consideration will be given them in this chapter. Greater emphasis, however, will be put on the ideas of Whitman and on Burroughs' own thought as each from his own horizon suggested in some degree metaphysical notions of Whitehead. Whitman's ". . . direct joy in the apprehension of things which lie around us"[4] was for Whitehead one of the attractions in his poetry. There is no evidence that he read Burroughs, but the two were not far apart in their estimates of Whitman. To Burroughs, Whitman as a poet of the cosmos was unparalleled; and to Whitehead he was one of the few great world poets.[5]

By the great world current in which he found Whitman, Burroughs meant something more than the rise of naturalism or of modern science. Added to science he names three other streams of global influence in Whitman's poetry: democracy, humanitarianism, and a new religion. All four enter into the first sociological section of Whitehead's *Adventures of Ideas*. Democracy and humanitarianism, he sees, are already intertwined; science and religion, he had insisted earlier, should also be united. It is with the possible union of these two latter streams that this study is largely concerned. Burroughs and Whitman would both see science and religion at one: the former leaning more strongly toward naturalism and science; the latter, toward religion or the position of a mystic. The slight strain of mysticism in Burroughs came from his absorbing interest in nature; his intimate relations with the birds gave meaning to his life. Any true lover of nature, he declares, must show an element of mysticism. This he sees, for instance, in Emerson. But the most convincing appeal of mysticism came to him from the scientists. In Lamarck he read that the divinity shaping the ends of organisms is "an inward perfecting principle";[6] in his contemporary, Tyndall, that matter is ". . . at bottom essentially mystical and transcendental."[7] Whitman's mysticism, pervasive throughout his writing, has been called cosmic consciousness. It is dynamic rather than passive, and recognizes throughout organic life a cosmic self akin to the meaning of the Hindu phrase "thou art it" or to Professor Hocking's inter-subjective *thou art*, which he identifies with God in man.[8]

As Burroughs' later essays are deeply concerned with the mystery of being, his interest in Whitman's mystical thought may be understood; but it is natural that he should give special attention to Whitman's responses to the scientific discoveries of his time. Burroughs finds Whitman like Tennyson absorbing and reproducing emotionally the sci-

ence of his day. He ". . . makes me feel," Burroughs declares, "how the ground I walk upon is a part of the solar
system,"[9] the earth as a celestial body thus sharing the glory
of the heavens. From "A Song of the Rolling Earth," Burroughs quotes

The divine ship sails the divine seas.

He calls Whitman ". . . astronomer, geologist, biologist all in
one, . . ."[10] Yet the poet sings more from the inspiration of
science than from exact knowledge. His fine lines in "Song
of Myself" on the evolution of man, coming four years
before *Origin of Species,* excited Burroughs' admiration.

Rise after rise bow the phantoms behind me,

was a favorite verse which he often cited. "It is only by
regarding man as a part of nature," Burroughs observes, "as
the outcome of the same vital forces underfoot and over-
head that the plants and animals are, that we can find God
in the world."[11]

It is the idea of God in the world, in all that lives, but
particularly in the heart of man, that affects most profoundly
the message of *Leaves of Grass.* Through science Whitman
enters but an area of his dwelling; his mystic vision goes
beyond in surveying the *path between reality and the soul.*[12]
Before the first edition of his poems in 1855, he had almost
certainly read the essays in Emerson's *Representative Men*
among those that brought his simmering ideas to a boil;
and he could hardly have missed Emerson's reference to
Swedenborg's *Animal Kingdom.* "It was written with the
highest end," Emerson noted, "to put science and soul, long
estranged from each other at one again." In Whitman's 1876
Preface, he stresses the thought that the eternal soul of man
is a higher fact than "the flights of science." "The supreme
and final science," he had said in his Preface of 1872, "is the
science of God. . . ." Beyond all the transformations of man
through the ages, poetically rendered in "Song of Myself" is
his climactic stand with his "robust soul."

Whitman's position as a mystic needs perhaps at this point further clarification. Professor Gay Allen has cited Bertrand Russell on the central ideas of most mystics,[13] which may be found rather clearly illustrated in Whitman. The first is insight—knowledge obtained by intuition. Great truths in Whitman, Burroughs asserts, are intuitive.[14] This insight in Whitman, called by Dr. Bucke cosmic consciousness, is supported to a degree by the second idea of unity—plurality and division being illusory. Whitman sees this unity through the universal soul immanent in man and the natural world. Like most mystics a monist, he diverges from Whitehead in this respect. In "Crossing Brooklyn Ferry" he speaks of himself as "struck from the float" (or oversoul), and given identity by his body; only through his body has he absolutely appeared. This merging of the spiritual and physical in identity, and their inseparableness are Whitman's reasons, Burroughs shows, for giving equal importance to body and soul. The third idea—unreality of Time and Space to the soul—is suggested in "Song of Myself" as the poet is afoot with his vision in other places and in earlier times. The final notion that evil is mere appearance may seem to be contradicted by various passages in *Leaves of Grass;* but to Whitman, Burroughs indicates in his *Study* of the poet, "evil is an unripe kind of good."[15] "Only the good," Whitman claims, "is universal."[16] Only that has a permanent value.

Like both Burroughs and Whitman, Whitehead was to see the deep significance of science and religion in the current of world history, and the importance of harmony between the two. He finds science inadequate, as does Burroughs, in arriving at truth. Burroughs would turn to philosophy for interpretation of eternal verities, but his search for God continues throughout his life. "The reaction of human nature to its search for God"[17] Whitehead calls religion—repeated visions of God that have brought out the noblest in man. His own reaction to this search is his concept of the dipolar nature of God in the world, awakening man to action by persuasion and motivation. Whether through the immanence of the past, in its relation to His consequent nature, or through transcendence in connection with His primordial nature, the lure for feeling is at work. Arising as a subjective aim from transcendence, the lure is not unlike Lamarck's inner perfecting principle, which, though denied as purpose by Darwin, Burroughs does not find incompatible with the theory of evolution. Man, rooted in nature, Whitman implies, must expand with an expanding universe; yet his soul, he insists, is highest guide. That there is an order of nature recognized by man, Whitehead stresses as strongest evidence of a supreme author of the cosmos; and to know Him means an intermingling of the spirit and the senses. The inter-relation and interaction of the physical and mental as demonstrated in the philosophy of organism point to a basic harmony in the findings of science and metaphysics.

A long standing conflict between science and religion presupposes an indifference to such a study of thought as we are making on the subject of God in the world. With the agreement of science and religion the thought becomes reality as it did for Whitehead and for Whitman, and somewhat less definitely for Burroughs. From both Goethe and Emerson, however, Burroughs received spiritual assurance on principles we have seen underlying Whitehead's philosophy of organism; and these principles are upheld with greater vigor in the poetry of Whitman, which Burroughs discusses in one book and two essays of his works, and mentions or quotes frequently throughout his twenty-three volumes.

To process, immanence, relatedness, interfusion, creativity, and transition then we shall turn again as entering into the world current of thought in support of science and of religion and of their possible agreement. With Burroughs as with Whitehead process involves both being and becoming. The principle of process, Whitehead notes, is that its being is constituted by how it becomes. The temporal things arise by participation in things that are eternal; thus the importance of eternal objects in process. Burroughs' references to constant becoming in the natural world do not preclude the idea of a Creative Energy which he identifies with the Infinite or God. He quotes Emerson as loving nothing "but what now is and is becoming,"[18] but recognizes too that for Emerson whatever becomes is dependent upon power given it by the Eternal. Power and form were to Emerson the permanent and the temporal united in process. In Emerson's claim that the eternal tendency is to the good of the whole, Burroughs sees religion and science joining hands. Stages in process that Whitehead was to outline are merely suggested by Burroughs. "Action and reaction," he says in *Accepting the Universe,* "are the steps by which life ascends. Nature acts upon man and man reacts upon nature."[19]

Process in the natural world he would trace to life's origin, and finds in radio-activity mysteries of action and reaction that occupy his attention through much of the volume entitled *The Breath of Life.* Published in 1915, the book refers frequently to the work of Frederick Soddy, English chemist, who in 1921 was to receive the Nobel prize. From Soddy Burroughs gathers that radio-activity is the main-spring of the universe. In *Science and the Modern World* Whitehead finds underlying all process an eternal energy, which he seems at that time to associate with God. As Burroughs, quoting Emerson, notes that "the inorganic is dreaming of the organic,"[20] Whitehead, following process in both, sees stages approximately analogous. By re-enaction of the initial stage of process, Whitehead shows, the pattern of a living occasion is reiterated somewhat as the vibration or ebb and flow of energy in an electron is arrested in dis-continuous passage about the nucleus of an atom. Although Burroughs does not speak of the quantum theory discovered in 1900, from his discussion of the atom and its component parts; of the electron, its vibration of energy, and its dis-integration into light waves, he would understand, it ap-pears, Whitehead's tentative use of the quantum theory in explaining the organic theory of process.

Whitehead's analysis of process includes purpose or a subjective aim, and Burroughs earlier insists that organic development presupposes purpose. Molecules within the living body he sees obeying some law other than chance.[21]

Yet he is quite free, he admits, from the "taint of teleology" or the idea of God as designer of the universe; his emphasis like that of Goethe, Emerson, and Whitehead is rather on a self-creating order deriving its impulse from God or a pervading intelligence in nature.

Process, we have seen, may mean becoming by first perishing. "To perish," Whitehead says, "is to assume a new function in the process of generation."[22] This notion of the reality of non-being, which came from classical tradition, we find also in Burroughs. "Only in a live universe," he says, in "The Gospel of Nature," "could disease and death prevail. Death is a phase of life, a redistributing of the type." We are immortal, he adds in "The Natural Providence," through our part in creative energy. "The universal mind does not die, the universal life does not go out."[23] It remains, as Whitehead would claim, in the guise of objective immortality.

Set apart from Burroughs, Goethe, and Emerson by his definite position as a mystic, Whitman needs separate treatment as we consider his thought suggesting in some measure that of Whitehead. Knowing Whitehead's enjoyment in reading Whitman and the high opinion he held of Whitman's work, would lend weight to the thought of kinship in their ideas. To pantheism we have found Whitehead definitely objecting; yet in his insistence on the foundation of the world in aesthetic experience,[24] derived in turn from the immanence of God, he is not far from the thinking of Whitman. For Whitehead the aesthetic experience reflects the notion of process as it advances into novelty and value; it begins with the creative impulse from the lure and ends with a goal becoming determinate in an aesthetic fact. This becoming, from the beginning of the world, has meant the achievement of unity out of diversity, of identity realized in contrasts. The universal self that Whitman celebrates in *Leaves of Grass* is in its cosmic and mystic evolution a gradual approach to unity from diverse experience. The poet's aesthetic point of view in realizing similitude in dissimilitude appears again and again as in his concept of body and soul and of good and evil. The mystic trumpeter's "glad, exulting, culminating song" is of the soul, supreme as spirit in man feeling the joys of heaven upon earth. With Whitman as with Whitehead the creative process issues from and flows toward the immanence of God.

Whitman, Whitehead remarks, ". . . brought something into poetry that was never there before. Much of what he says is so new that he even had to invent a form for saying it."[25] The poet's reiteration of words and phrases, wave upon wave, to press home his meaning, was due no doubt in part to the organic theory stemming from German idealism. But there is also some resemblance to Whitehead's stress on organic re-enaction in process to gain intensity that will end in value. The scientific background of the poet's cosmic self —his organic evolution—is echoed and re-echoed as well as the ideals inherent in the American dream—all a part of the rôle Whitman plays. Radio-activity and the quantum theory came too late for his horizon; but throughout his book the self he sings must be alive as a part of the natural world. There must be self-enjoyment and purpose as in the philosophy of organism.

"Process," Whitehead says in *Science and the Modern World*, "brings latencies into being—an awakening to action he has indicated by his use of appetition. Lines in "Song of Myself," which Burroughs reiterates, have a comparable meaning:

Urge and urge and urge
Always the procreant urge of the world

Whitman's "Song of Joys" reflects an experiencing of values such as Whitehead finds in the self-enjoyment of an occasion. The term *occasion* might indeed be applied to the various experiences in *Leaves of Grass*, many of them on a magnified scale as Whitman, the subject, absorbs the life of his times. An historic route of occasions that makes for personality with Whitehead is paralleled in "Song of Myself" by the poet's perpetual journey,

Not I, not anyone else can travel that road for you
You must travel it for yourself

"There is no stoppage," Whitman insists, but "whatever sat-
isfies the soul is truth";[26] and such satisfaction terminating
an occasion in the philosophy of organism clinches value.
Enjoyment for Whitehead includes purpose; and to Whitman "Purpose entire and several"[27] must promote all becoming throughout the natural world including man. Purpose
has then not only an individual but a universal significance.
Within the universe he sees

Forms, objects, growths, humanities, to spiritual images
    ripening

"The soul," he insists, "is above all science, and finds the
partial to the permanent flowing."

For it the real to the ideal tends.[28]

Stressing the divine average, a self-hood universal in its
application, Whitman feels that "the crowning growth of
the United States is to be spiritual and heroic."[29] The Civil
War years strengthen his conviction. Step by step life is for
him a mystic as well as a cosmic evolution. In a universe
that Whitehead sees "on one side . . . physically wasting, on
the other side . . . spiritually ascending,"[30] he believes that
God within the world points to a trend toward order, toward a possible kingdom of heaven upon earth. More explicit than Whitehead on personal immortality, Whitman
sings on the theme of death his most triumphant note. He
feels life to be "surely going somewhere," and awaits a new
spiritual existence.

Immanence is the second principle supporting the idea
of God in the world. Burroughs declares in *Time and
Change* that God's immanence in the universe is part of his
scientific faith. "The power we call God," he asserts, "does
not sustain a mechanical or secondary relation to the universe, but is vital in it, or one with it. . . . The Infinite is

immanent in this universe."[31] Here he is close to Whitehead, and finds Goethe substantiating his statement. He
quotes from Goethe's autobiography: ". . . the persuasion
that a great producing, regulating, and conducting Being
conceals himself, as it were, behind nature, to make himself
comprehensible to us—such a conviction forces itself upon
every one."[32] In Burroughs' last paper "Facing the Mystery,"
his idea of immanence approaches Whitehead's notion of
objective immortality, "You and I perish," Burroughs reasons, "but something goes out or may go out from us that
will help forward a higher type of mankind."

Tyndall and Emerson, to whom Tyndall felt greatly indebted, suggested to Burroughs the mystic character of
immanence. From Emerson he quotes, "Nature is saturated
with deity."[33] To Tyndall more than to any other scientist
Burroughs owes his belief in the mystic and transcendental
character of atoms as the basis of all life. "The more by
searching," he writes, "we find out the true inwardness of
matter, the nearer we find ourselves to the borderland of
the unknowable, the transcendental, the incalculable."[34]
Calling himself an inborn naturalist and an inborn idealist,
Burroughs finds whatever is natural to be divine. There is a
strain of mysticism, we have found him insisting, in all true
nature lovers. The religious spirit that Whitehead sees
immanent in the world, "gives meaning to all that passes
and yet eludes apprehension."[35] We must always include
God, he maintains, in accounting for the derivation of the
physical world. To Burroughs the forces of inorganic nature
supporting life and at times destroying it, are a baffling
problem; yet the gradual recognition of the electrical basis
of the universe as energy, had in his time strengthened his
conclusion that inorganic and organic nature are regulated
by a cosmic mind beyond human understanding. Like
Whitehead later he sees no lasting reasons for a conflict
between religion and science.

Immanence in the various meanings given it by Whitehead is true for Whitman as for Burroughs. At the same
time immanence in its mystical sense is to him more important than in the meaning used by science. The immanence

of the past in the present, however, he clearly indicates. "I raise the present on the past," he says in one of his Inscriptions, and asserts the growth of the present out of the past in "Passage to India" and in "The Prayer of Columbus." But "the urge, the ardor, the unconquerable will" of Columbus all show the immanence of God transcendent in pointing to potentiality and in supporting the explorer's activities. Like Emerson and like Whitehead, Whitman finds science in looking ever for facts often misses a greater truth.

Everything, he believed, as did Goethe, had a soul; but Whitman is the more emphatic, as in "To Think of Time,"

> I swear I think now that everything without exemption has an eternal soul!

Whitman asserts his doctrine of souls or spiritual seeds in "Eidolons," one of the Inscriptions to *Leaves of Grass*.

> The old, old urge
> Based on the ancient pinnacles, lo, newer, higher pinnacles
> From science and the modern still impell'd
> The old, old urge, eidolons

Such images or souls of objects harbored in man would make for his spiritual growth.[36] This is seen in Whitman's poem, "There Was a Child Went Forth."

> The early lilacs became part of that child,
> And grass and white and red morning glories, and white and red clover, and the song of the phoebe-bird,

But the poet is most interested in immanence of spirit in the soul of man, "struck from the float" and given individuality or identity through the body. The general spiritual essence designated as the "float" in "Crossing Brooklyn Ferry" and elsewhere, becomes in "Chanting the Square Deific,"

Santa Spirita, breather, life
. . .
Essence of forms, life of the real identities, permanent, positive,

The idea that all life is included in Santa Spirita, called by Whitman the general soul, suggests the Neo-Platonic theory of emanation, important to Emerson in seeing not only God in the world but the world in God. This is Whitehead's view at the conclusion of *Process and Reality;* yet he did not accept the idea of emanation. Whitman's use of the chemical term "float, forever held in solution" as symbol for God in the world, may, however, have attracted his attention as did Shelley's use of images from science in "Prometheus Unbound."[37] The word "float" was possibly suggested to Whitman from a sentence in Emerson's essay "Spiritual Laws," "Place yourself in the middle of the stream of power and wisdom which animates all whom it floats. . . ."[38]

These examples of a mystic immanence: images from nature developing the soul; and the immanence of Santa Spirita or the float in identities disintegrated yet held in solution, indicate some resemblance to and some divergence from the lure for feeling. Whitehead's lure as eternal object made everlasting in objective immortality, attracts like the lilac, the grass, and the phoebe bird. Indeed in *Nature and Life* he notes that "this experienced world . . . lies at the base of the soul's existence."[39] But his rejection of the Neo-Platonic World Soul, in some respects like Whitman's "float" leads to a different concept of an entity in the making from that of Whitman's: a disintegrated self through emanation "struck from the float." Whitman too would have agreed only in part with Whitehead's notion of value enduring in objective immortality. Stating plainly that only the good is universal or endures but intent on man's mystic evolution, Whitman would not be satisfied with such immortality as the "choir invisible" or memory gives. We are surely going somewhere, he insists, somewhere beyond time and space.

On the subject of relatedness as well as that of process

and of immanence, Burroughs, though sympathetic with
Whitman's point of view, is more attracted by scientific
conclusions than by mystical announcements. A recurrent
theme in Burroughs' essays is man's relatedness to nature
in its various aspects. "We are adjusted to the sphere" [in
which we live], he says, "not it to us." And "our most constant and vital relation to the world . . ." he notes, is chemical, since we could not exist without oxygen.[40] Darwin and
other scientists had taught Burroughs that man is a part of
nature; but Tyndall, perhaps more than any other, that man
is not an irreconcilable part. And to Emerson, Burroughs
refers as exalting the idea of "our kinship with the whole
of nature."[41] A deep sense of this relationship Emerson in
turn owed to Goethe. Man's reason, Goethe believed, and
on this point was quoted twice by Burroughs, may participate in a higher reason behind the production of nature. It
is the plasticity of nature, we have seen, that Whitehead
finds exhibited in its most intense form in man. Thus the
protean character of creativity by which entities enter into
new phases of themselves, is more completely illustrated in
higher phases of development than in natural processes.

Man's relatedness to nature as a part of it supports the
idea of matter and mind as one. This notion, acclaimed by
Goethe and by Emerson, is reiterated by Burroughs. "The
more we know matter," he asserts, "the more we know
mind; the more we know nature, the more we know God;
the more familiar we are with earth forces, the more intimate will be our acquaintance with the celestial forces."[42]
The unity of body and spirit could not be denied, he
claims, if we understand our relations to the Cosmos. These
conclusions would seem to have come in part from Burroughs' meditations on Lamarck's "inner perfecting principle" and on Tyndall's speculations as to the transcendental
character of atoms; in part, no doubt, from conversations
with Whitman. Whitehead's analysis of the actual occasion,
his unit of process, leads to his conclusions that each occasion unites its physical inheritance from the past with its
mental reaction in a drive toward self-formation.[43] Unity of
mind and matter is thus in a sense established.

The theory of the world's beauty and harmony as a unit in which all details are a part, underlies concepts of relatedness, we have seen, in the work of Goethe and of Emerson. Burroughs quotes from Emerson, "Nothing is beautiful alone. Nothing but is beautiful in the whole." The thought of the poem "Each and All" illustrating this statement parallels an earlier quotation from Goethe. "Every creature sundered from its natural surroundings . . . and brought into strange company, makes an unpleasant impression on us. . . ."[44] Emerson's sea shells lose their freshness of pearl when taken from the froth of the waves, and the music of the songster is stilled in the captivity of a cage. In line with this view is Whitehead's category of subjective unity; it is identified, he indicates, with the "doctrine of pre-established harmony." This involves a careful balancing of contrasting elements to secure a final effect of unity and the attainment of symmetry and truth. The unification of the world in order and value is thus constantly renewed.[45]

In his poem "On the Beach at Night Alone" Whitman looks up at the stars and sees that "a vast similitude interlocks all." Burroughs has quoted him on this sense of relatedness which ". . . spans all objects of the universe and compactly holds and encloses them."[46] Yet the riddles of the cosmos, which Whitman finds mirrored in man, he does not, Burroughs notes, like Lucretius, try to solve, but would encompass the universe so far as possible by putting his arms around his fellow man.[47] Particularly appealing to Burroughs is Whitman's feeling of kinship with the natural world. "To me," the poet says in "Song of Myself," "the converging objects of the universe perpetually flow." To Whitehead the initial stage of process shows this relatedness in the impact of a unified group of objects on the prehending subject. Wordsworth was such a subject as his attention was arrested in a lonely spot by daffodils dancing in the breeze.

In *Democratic Vistas* the idealism of Whitman's democracy shows the principles of relatedness and equality combined with his feeling, derived from Emerson, for the infinitude of man. Great men arise from pride in identity and

are needed for the success of democracy; but the ideas of
the infinitude of man and of equality are harmonized
through relatedness, which comes obviously from the common origin of souls in Santa Spirita or God in the world.
"This America," Whitman asserts in "By Blue Ontario's
Shore," "is only you and me." But the *you* and *me* embody
the many linked with or related to the One. "Produce great
Persons," Whitman urges in the same poem, "the rest follows." Whitman's humanitarian ideals are linked with democracy in their inclusion of brotherhood, equality, and
freedom.[48] The spiritual relatedness which Whitman finds
in religion, calling God the "Comrade Perfect" and "Elder
Brother," Whitehead also finds in the relation of God to
man as the "Fellow Sufferer" and "Great Companion."

Relatedness is clearly connected with the unity and
harmony of the universe; it would seem also to have a
bearing on the interaction of various entities, often through
contrast, in the concrescence of a living occasion. To this
concrescence Whitehead applies the term "fluency"; the
growing together of contributing elements in the becoming
of an actual entity, he would also see as interfusion.[49] In its
suggestion of interweaving elements that in their function
are dynamic, motivated by the power of the lure, interfusion merits separate attention. Without arriving at a
theory of concrescence, Burroughs was yet strongly convinced of the inter-relation and inter-dependence of the
whole living world, pervaded, as he believed, by a cosmic
mind. He sees also the constant interaction of inorganic
and organic nature, and would have agreed with Whitehead on such interplay in the whirling of molecules within
the living body.

Interfusion of time is implied by Whitehead in his chapters on "Past, Present, and Future," and on "Appearance
and Reality" in *Adventures of Ideas;* here the connection of
the present to its past and its future is very close. Goethe
and Emerson also felt this correlation and are followed by
Burroughs. The interfusion of time and the interweaving of
other relationships result for Goethe in a universal unity.
Burroughs speaks of him as living "in the whole,"[50] and sees

with him and Emerson that a world of intertwining relationships makes isolation impossible. His ideas on inter-
relationship are expressed definitely in "A Naturalist's View
of Life."

> Threads of relation, visible and invisible—chemical,
> mechanical, electric, magnetic, solar, lunar, stellar, geo-
> logic, biologic—forming an intricate web of subtle forces
> and influences, bind all things, living and dead, into a
> cosmic unity.[51]

Similar convictions led Whitehead to deny validity to the
theory of simple location and to say that "in a certain sense
everything is everywhere at all times." Nature's roads, Burroughs had remarked earlier, "are roads to everywhere. They
may lead you to your own garden, or to the North Pole, or
to fixed stars, or may end where they began."[52] But an event
after all, to Whitehead, has singularity and has value in
proportion to the harmony of its parts merged through
concrescence into a completed unity.

Emerson and Goethe both find a kind of spiritual interfusion in the relation between man and nature. In his essay
on Swedenborg, Emerson had called the human body an
instrument through which the soul is fed; and Burroughs,
commenting on Emerson's clarity in viewing Swedenborg's
theories, adds that ". . . the spiritual has its roots in the
carnal."[53] This is evident in Whitehead's analysis of process
and creativity; conceptual feelings arise from prehensions
of the physical world. Sympathy and insight into nature
come, Emerson had suggested, "by making one's self a
centre for nature." In Burroughs' "Gospel of Nature" he
finds learning the ways of the birds brings a spiritual up-
lift. "To take the birds out of my life," he writes, "would
be like lopping off so many branches from the trees; there is
so much less surface of leafage to absorb the sunlight and
bring my spirits in contact with the vital currents."[54] We
have here an illustration of what Whitehead would call
mutual immanence, to which he would add a doctrine of
internal relations, showing that ". . . characters of the

relevant things in nature [and man is included] are the outcome of their interconnections, and their interconnections are the outcome of their characters."[55] It is only through the highest reason, Burroughs finds Goethe saying to Eckermann, that nature reveals herself to man: ". . . man must be capable of elevating himself to the highest Reason to come into that contact with the Divinity which manifests [itself] in the primitive phenomena. . . ."[56] Burroughs apparently agrees with Goethe and with Emerson that identification with nature might lead to an intuitive understanding of the divine power behind all life. We have already seen that Whitehead's early nature studies gave him an insight leading to his metaphysical conclusions.

It is always Burroughs' relations with nature that reveal in him a mystic strain, and that must have contributed much to his years of comradeship with Whitman. Burroughs recognizes Whitman's insight, like that of Emerson, into what is divine and universal ". . . in the common and near at hand."[57] As poet of the Kosmos, Whitman is to Burroughs uniquely composite. The word "composite" Burroughs had apparently taken from Whitman's claim for *Leaves of Grass* in his Preface of 1876—"that all my pieces . . . are only of use and value . . . as an interpenetrating, composite, inseparable unity." That unity is the poet's personality. Tallying with the times in which he lived, he is indeed a part of all that he has met, and it is hardly possible to grasp what he as poet of the Kosmos, would absorb in himself.

> I am an acme of things accomplished and I an encloser of things to be
>
> . . .
>
> I am large, I contain multitudes

he claims in "Song of Myself";[58] and in "*Salut au Monde*" he absorbs within himself all the wonders of the globe: its geography, natural resources, and inhabitants; with all he feels a divine rapport. In shorter poems such as "There was a Child Went Forth" and "Weave in, My Hardy Life" he shows the intertwining of vital experiences. The most impressive interweaving of elements may be found in his two finest poems on death. In "Out of the Cradle Endlessly Rocking" the trio—boy, bird, and sea—interact dramatically as involved in the poet's chosen theme; and in the elegy on Lincoln, "lilac and star and bird twined with the chant of my soul" brings the poem to a conclusion of solemnity and beauty.

Whitehead's interest in Whitman must have been largely because he was a poet of the cosmos, for in shaping his philosophy of organism, he was seeking a tentative theory of creation. Both poet and philosopher, envisaging the universe and all life within it, must have felt in the total ensemble not only interfusion or interaction but a slowly expanding evolution of the spirit. For Whitehead, who sees in the objective immortality of the world nothing without value, the soul plays a deeply significant rôle as for Whitman, who sees something more immortal than the stars in the spirit's insatiate desire to continue beyond present horizons.[59] The evolution of the soul, however, does not lead Whitehead, like Whitman, to the apotheosis of man; nor in this respect was the poet followed by Burroughs. The lure in Whitehead's last book becomes rather the indwelling Eros urging the soul toward purposeful ends, which must mean the dynamic merging of itself in other living elements as new values are created.

Creativity or process in the large is basically the theory of novelty, but novelty attaining value only as conditioned by God. For Burroughs and later for Whitehead the atom and radio-activity are significant in throwing light on the creative process. Life has for Burroughs a connotation resembling that of Whitehead's creativity; and he is constantly seeking life's origin as somehow connected with the primal mind or an organizing principle. May not science, he queries, be discovering such a principle in looking inside the atom? The divine centre of which Goethe and Emerson both speak, Burroughs suggests, may there be found. The whirl of those minute particles attracting and repelling each other in what he calls a mystic dance, must have been guided by a primordial mind. Nature works, Burroughs says as Emerson, probably influenced by Goethe, had said earlier, ". . . by unfolding and ever unfolding, or developing out of latent powers and possibilities. . . ."[60]

Such powers and possibilities Whitehead calls potentialities for becoming. What Burroughs refers to as primal mind, Whitehead would term in *Science and the Modern World* "an underlying eternal energy," which he sees embodied in natural occurrences.[61] His description of the way in which an atomic occasion entertains its energy in accordance with the theory of continuity or of quanta, indicates a possible parallel to a doctrine of continuity or of individuality in occasions of human experience. If the flux of energy is favored rather than the quanta; that is, its flow from the past and its transmission to the future rather than the measure of its flow, continuity or inheritance from the past will be dominant over individuality. In the reverse situation individuality rather than conformity will be supreme, in some sense suggesting the intensity of satisfaction allied with the creation of novelty.[62] These conclusions help to explain Whitehead's meaning when he says, ". . . final causation and atomism are interconnected philosophical principles."[63]

Within the atom the electron's absorption of energy as it moves from an inner to an outer orbit,[64] presents a picture bearing some resemblance to the idea of appropriation, which both Goethe and Emerson regarded as an important factor in the creative process. And appropriation Whitehead was later to identify with prehension. It is illustrated most clearly in man as he takes to himself material for which he has a special concern. This for Burroughs was nature, and from his earliest book, *Wake Robin,* he is alert to discover nature's secrets. His method suggests in some measure Whitehead's theory of creativity, involving the lure for feeling, appropriation, and a subjective aim. Burroughs must have with nature "an emotional intercourse," "absorb her, and reproduce her tinged with the colors of the spirit."[65] "We find God," he writes, as had also Goethe and Emerson, ". . . in the common, the near, always present, always active, always creating the world anew."[66] To understand the majesty and meaning of nature, he says, must require

intuition, a reaching forth of the spirit as Goethe had indicated. It was Burroughs' love of nature that drew to him
confidingly the wild creatures of woods and fields, and thus
he learned their ways. As illustrated in his poem "Waiting,"
his development, like Goethe's, implied an aggregation of
that with which he was most deeply concerned.

> Serene, I fold my hands and wait,
> Nor care for wind, nor tide, nor sea;
> I rave no more 'gainst Time or Fate,
> For lo! my own shall come to me.
>
> I stay my haste, I make delays,
> For what avails this eager pace?
> I stand amid the eternal ways,
> And what is mine shall know my face.[67]

Like Goethe too Burroughs not only appropriated nature
but reproduced her, "tinged with the colors of the spirit."
Both anticipated Whitehead in seeing the necessity of combining the concrete with the universal in the creative process. On the union in art of the factual and the ideal, Burroughs quotes Goethe: "The highest problem of any art is
to produce by semblance the illusion of some higher reality."[68] The need of combining factual knowledge with aesthetic and mystical interpretation, Burroughs emphasizes, if
we would understand the world as it stands related to our
higher instincts. As a clue to his meaning he gives a line
from Goethe's introduction to *"Gott und Welt"*: "There is a
universe within thee, as well—"[69] one, it is implied, in
which man, inspired by God, or the lure for feeling, exer-
cises his power to create.

That universe, according to Whitman, is the soul; ". . . it
makes itself visible," he observes, as Goethe had earlier,
"only through matter."[70] Whitehead was to see the soul
growing out from physical experiences. In "Proud Music of
the Storm," it is to his soul that Whitman sings as whistling
winds and hum of forest trees, and roaring cataracts call up
the music of all times and places, the great operas, the

dance music of the nations, and hymns of all ages. Here is the aesthetic experience Whitehead stresses of contrasts under the identity of sound in nature and in art; and all this, the poet announces

> . . . led to thee O soul,
> All senses, shows and objects lead to thee,

The *pathway from reality to the soul* is then linked with the aesthetic order, the process of creating with the soul's advance into novelty. The symphonic movement of Whitman's verses has an elemental quality described by the poet himself as he compares his rhythms to the "recurrence of lesser and larger waves on the sea shore, rolling in without intermission and fitfully rising and falling."[71] Burroughs in his reaction has ". . . the impression of something dynamic, something akin to the vital forces of the organic world. . . ."[72] In "The Mystic Trumpeter" the music translated leads to joy, the normal state of the soul, to Wordsworth and Whitehead as well as to Whitman.

The universe within, Goethe feels, approximates the universe without so far as possible through the agency of creativity. Creation must start, Whitman claims, with ". . . reference to the ensemble of the world, and the compact truth of the world."[73] Whitehead's discussion of appearance and reality in *Adventures of Ideas* stresses the same point; the continual renewal and re-unification which he sees in the universe, must follow such a law for creation. Appropriation, or for Whitehead prehension, we have seen to be an early phase of creativity essential in the natural world and in man for the production of novelty. Since Burroughs had appropriated nature, feeling himself a part of it, he is particularly attracted to Whitman, who absorbed ". . . the spirit of nature through the visible objects of the universe. . . ."[74] By Whitman's cosmic sense of possession Burroughs is fascinated; he follows the poet on his quest, a "journey through the universe"; and feels through his poetry ". . . in touch with primal energies."[75]

This method of appropriation is evident in Whitman's

apparent purpose to make *Leaves of Grass* an epic of America, the hero, the modern man or cosmic self he celebrates.[76]
Burroughs could see what Whitman was attempting and could appreciate his need of identifying himself with everything American, of drawing "everything into himself like a maelstrom."[77] As he approaches his task in "Starting from Paumanok," the poet says

> I will sleep no more but arise
> You oceans that have been calm within me! how I feel you, fathomless, stirring, preparing unprecedented waves and storms.

Pride in and affection for democracy stimulate Whitman's artistic efforts, and bring the joy that he feels normal in all experience. It is a fusion of democratic and cosmic feeling that inspires him in "A Song of Joys,"

> O the joy of that vast elemental sympathy which only the human soul is capable of generating and emitting in steady and limitless floods.

As poet of the cosmos, Whitman must have exemplified to Whitehead the principle of novelty that has become value.

Value for Whitman, as in the philosophy of organism, is increased by intensity; ". . . from any fruition of success, no matter what," he affirms, "shall come forth something to make a greater struggle necessary." Burroughs sees satisfaction coming through effort only ". . . and then not for long."[78]
For Whitman the great end of struggle, transformed into joy, is achieving identity, is being *yourself*. Yet self-hood or self-creation, with him as with Whitehead has a general application; and there is a sense of the universal in the adventure and zest of realizing potentiality and value.

As Whitehead's lure reveals relatedness and guides concrescence or interfusion to satisfaction in the creation of value, it motivates transition or the passing from value attained in objective immortality to attainment of further value in the concrescence of a new occasion. Transition then is a basic activity we have seen to be closely allied with creativity. In the pervasive motion and change in the world, Burroughs finds, as had Whitehead, following Plato, imperfection reaching toward something higher. This ascending effort of the universe, Burroughs maintains, is the only sound view. Guided by contemporary science, he regards the atom as a centre of ever-moving energy extending to the outermost bounds of the universe. But the impelling power that gives direction to atoms, purpose to matter, and to the "one seething welter of modes of motion"[79] in the universe, he sees also giving vent to the actions of living beings like ourselves. Yet it is only as we look back from continuous development or transition that we are conscious of the levels we have passed in reaching new horizons. More than once Burroughs quotes Whitman on the spirit's leveling one lift "to pass and continue beyond."[80] In the philosophy of organism, it must be kept in mind, however, that an impelling power gives place to one that is persuasive in the creative advance of life.

In the progress of the world, then, Burroughs writes, motion may seem invisible, but moving power is never absent. It is behind motion or activity that may often be concealed in the organic or inorganic world. Consider, for instance, the invisible opening of blossoms to the sun, which the microscope brings clearly before our eyes. Power behind possibly invisible motion, recognized in electric energy, Burroughs finds Emerson identifying with evolution. Transition or passage then, whether visible or not, in mass or molecular activity, is an eternal flux. Science, Burroughs says, sees it everywhere, ". . . motion within motion . . . currents and countercurrents everywhere, ceaseless change everywhere. . . ."[81] Goethe had called this eternal flux in his day metamorphosis—an idea reiterated by Emerson.

Turning specifically to human experience, we have found Whitman saying in "Song of Myself," "I tramp a perpetual journey," one, as we have seen, comparable to the development of personality in the philosophy of organism. "All below duly travel'd," the poet claims, "and still I mount and mount." It is all part of Whitman's idea of mystic evolution—"the journey of man through countless ages." And though to the poet, man is the centre of interest in the universe, his advance is also promoted by his relation to the unceasing flux and transition of all things.

> To me the converging objects of the universe perpetually flow
> All are written to me, and I must get what the writing means.[82]

The tallying of Whitman's cosmic self with what goes on in the universe, we have seen to be a central part of his plan for *Leaves of Grass*; nowhere does he depict more vividly an experience shared by multitudes than in "Crossing Brooklyn Ferry." A symbolic picture of man's transient earthly passage, the crossing involves physical objects that endure through time, and whose converging upon the poet will endear him to readers having a similar experience some hundred years hence. The *sunset clouds,* the *crested waves,* the *seagulls,* the *hasting current,* the *flags of all nations*— all furnish their *parts toward eternity,* their *parts toward* the *soul.* Some years later Whitehead was to speak of the experienced world as lying "at the base of the soul's existence."[83] In the life of the soul actual entities or living occasions play their part in the historic route that establishes personal identity. Transition from publicity to private experience may lead to attainment of value which is again transmitted to the world as objective immortality. Something more than this was meant by Emerson in his later years when he asserted, "We are immortal by force of transits." And in "Passage to India" of 1871, Whitman is confident of something beyond present knowledge and experience.

> O my brave soul!
> O farther, farther sail!
> O daring joy, but safe! are they not all the seas of God?
> O farther, farther, farther sail!

In a later poem in memory of a talk with his friend, Mrs.
Gilchrist, he repeats an earlier assurance:

> The world, the race, the soul—in space and time the
>   universe,
> All bound as is befitting each—all going somewhere.

Whitman's creative impulse

The old, old urge
. . .
From science and the modern world impell'd,

is not unlike that of Goethe and of Emerson, whose assur-
ances of God in the world so impress Burroughs. All four
would seem to anticipate Whitehead in his firm conviction
that a power behind the processes of the natural world and
higher phases of experience must be recognized by science
and by philosophy. A naturalist in contrast to Whitman as
mystic, Burroughs could not follow him in his apotheosis of
the human soul; but he agreed with Whitman on the need
of harmony between science and religion. In their spiritual
rapport with all forms of life, both, Professor Hocking might
say, were touching "the near edge" of what he called God.[84]
Affirming the presence of a primal mind or God within
the world, they were not far from Whitehead's concept of
the lure for feeling. As a centre for generally accepted principles to be later articulated in the philosophy of organism,
the lure seems to have found a response in Burroughs and
in Whitman as well as in Goethe and in Emerson. The
thought of Whitehead, deeper and broader in its range than
that of Burroughs and of Whitman, is yet akin to their own.

v

WORDSWORTH AND WHITEHEAD ON
THE CREATIVE PROCESS

Admirers of Whitehead who know him best have suggested that Wordsworth had possibly a greater influence upon him than anyone except Plato.[1] Nowhere apparently has Whitehead admitted such an influence, as he has that of Plato and Locke and that of William James, Bergson, and Alexander among traditional and contemporary philosophers. But he had a predilection for poetry, and attributes to the great poets philosophical importance. They capture uniquely, he says, "a fragrance of experience"; and ". . . express deep intuitions of mankind penetrating into what is universal in concrete fact."[2] As observers of nature both Wordsworth and Whitehead ascribed to animate and inanimate life a degree of feeling or satisfaction in the course of being and becoming. Like the poet, Whitehead must have found "joy in widest commonalty spread."[3] The multiplication table, he noted at one time ". . . is no good to the realist. It shuts him up with Plato's ideas out of space and out of time" when ". . . like Wordsworth and the rest of us he wants to hear the throstle sing."[4]

It was curiously during Whitehead's early activity as a mathematician that he was reading most intensively the poetry of Wordsworth. No diaries or letters exist to substantiate this statement; the evidence comes from members of the family. "He would read *The Prelude,*" said his daughter, "as if it were the Bible, poring over the meaning of various passages." And at the same time his chief interest, always an important one, was mathematics; his philosophical ideas were then in the germ.[5] Since *The Prelude* is the

work of Wordsworth to which Whitehead gave most attention, our aim in this study is to determine mainly what he
found there which is most akin to his own thought as seen
in the basic metaphysical concepts underlying the philosophy of organism. To discuss in detail the categoreal scheme
of that philosophy would not appear to serve our purpose.

The metaphysical concepts of Whitehead which are
stressed as the basis of his philosophy by Professor Lowe, are
four: creativity, eternal objects, actual occasions, and prehensions. These are to be further understood by their inter-
connections through the non-temporal formative influence
of God.[6] Whitehead applies his metaphysical system to all
forms of life; but here the application will be limited to
higher phases of experience such as the processes of a poet's
mind in Wordsworth's *Prelude*. And although in Whitehead's metaphysical scheme consciousness is given a sub-
ordinate position, it must be considered here as he admits it
to be, "the crown of experience."[7]

Of the four basic concepts mentioned above, Whitehead
names creativity as the essential, ultimate principle of life
guided by divine direction to an increase of novelties in an
advancing universe. Through conceptual feelings derived
from God, selection and value enter into a world of otherwise indiscriminate productivity. Closely allied with creativity is "the realm of ideal entities" or eternal objects, a second
basic concept including forms or patterns, sounds, smells,
and feelings of unlimited range. These have a double function as potentially ingredient in the actual world about us
and conceptually possible in our mental operations or perceptions. Eternal objects, Whitehead says, participate in all
actual things according to a certain degree of relevance.[8]
The form of a sphere, for instance, is more completely
exemplified in a ball than in an apple. As creativity is the
ultimate principle of life, a third concept, the actual occasion or process of becoming, is the unit of creativity. "The
actual world is built up," Whitehead tells us, "of actual occasions."[9] And a basic factor in this process of becoming is
the fourth concept, the prehension, involving concern of an
active subject for a thing or for objects provoking this spe-

cial concern.[10] In the completion of a process or an actual occasion all four concepts are involved, and creation is accomplished through the combined power of conceptual and physical processes—of mental operations and the world.

God enters into the process as the "principle of concretion" without which there could be no emergence of value.[11] Through Him as a concrescent unity of conceptual feeling including all eternal objects comes the lure for feeling, then the subjective aim, which ends in accomplishment and satisfaction. This lure Whitehead calls "the germ of mind."[12] Wordsworth apparently thinks of the poet's mind as growing by feeding on infinity, a term which he associates with deity.[13] His announcement in "The Recluse" of his high argument in *The Prelude* and *The Excursion* is in line with Whitehead's basic ideas on creativity in his metaphysical system. Wordsworth sees as does Whitehead the mind and the world closely related in

. . . creation (by no lower name
Can it be called) which they with blended might
Accomplish:—this our high argument.[14]

The idea of creativity then underlying Wordsworth's autobiographical poem, *The Prelude*, would seem to be the main reason for its attraction to Whitehead. Regarding influence, however, Whitehead said once to a friend that where his ideas came from was simply a matter of one man's psychological history. The thing to do was to explore the applicability of these ideas.[15] In following that suggestion, an application of his analysis of process[16] to one of the poet's short poems created by the blended might of mind and nature may help to clarify the interaction of the basic concepts of Whitehead's metaphysics and at the same time serve to show some similarity of approach, on the part of philosopher and poet, to the creative process.

The composition of Wordsworth's poem, "The Green Linnet," in the mind of the poet we may consider the actual occasion in process of becoming. The process over, the poem takes its place as a novelty in the objective immortality of the world. The initial stage of the process is that of reception or responsiveness. The mind of the poet as subject receives the objective world about him with a pure physical prehension, all his senses alert, as he sits in the sequestered nook of his orchard. He feels the character of life awakening in the spring, and recognizes the individual tokens of trees, blossoms, birds, butterflies, and the linnet. All this has not yet been absorbed into what Whitehead calls "private immediacy" or subjective aim. This comes with the second supplemental stage divided into two phases: the appetitive or aesthetic phase and the intellectual or conscious phase. With the first phase of the supplemental stage in the process comes the lure for feeling, an emotional awareness that finds a degree of unity in the world about him through a permeating conceptual sense of the eternal object, joy. This emotional feeling, a positive prehension passing on to the poet from elements in the garden scene, reproduces in his mind the character of what is felt. Such a process of re-enaction and sharing is designated by Whitehead as a stage of creativity—"the throbbing emotion of the past hurling itself into a new transcendent fact."[17] He notes further that in the aesthetic phase of process there is an evocation of intensities, and the growth of intensity through contrasts and the integration of conceptual feelings. Wordsworth, in following the lure for feeling that results in a poem, finds sheer joy of *being* intensified by contrasts: joy of "brightest sunshine" and "unclouded weather" with the beginning of new life in the spring; joy of birds, butterflies, and flowers as paramours contrasted with that of the linnet, who is his own enjoyment; and joy evoked in his own mind by this concrescent world of spring time. If this joy as a pure potential is integrated with the tokens of animate life before him, intensity of feeling is increased.

The intellectual phase of the second stage in the becoming of an actual occasion presupposes consciousness—a private appreciation of experience which when completed becomes a public fact. Consciousness may be illustrated in Wordsworth's poem by the discriminating phrases expressing the linnet's sheer joy of being; for example, "the happiest guest in all this covert of the blest," "perched in ecstasies," and "brother of the dancing leaves." With the completion of the second stage of process comes the third of satisfaction, when the actual occasion or entity, completed by satisfying the urge to create or appetition, passes over into objective immortality as a poem or novelty added to the creative advance of the universe.

The study of Wordsworth's "Green Linnet" indicates the applicability of Whitehead's basic theories on process to the way the poem could have come into being. It also illustrates in a general way similar approaches of poet and philosopher to the problem of creation through the blended might of conceptual and physical process. A more detailed study of the creative process as outlined by Whitehead and revealed by Wordsworth in *The Prelude* will show further resemblances in philosophical approach.

In discussing the transmission and transmutation of feelings resulting in the concrescence or growing together of an actual occasion in its process of becoming, we shall include the powers of attraction between objects and subjects, appropriation through prehension, and the two pure modes of perception with their interplay which Whitehead calls symbolic reference. The mind then or subjective aim will be reviewed as agent and receiver: agent of God through the lure for feeling; and receiver of the world through prehension and perception. Interfusion of mind and the world, as Whitehead puts it, we shall see bearing a resemblance to the blending of mind and nature in the creative process, which becomes determinate for both philosopher and poet through the agency of deity. For the unity of feeling then achieved with the linking of efficient and final causation or for the satisfaction, according to Whitehead, in the completion of the actual occasion, we shall find some correspondence in *The Prelude*. This study will be concluded with an indication that Whitehead's theory of the creative process is akin to aesthetic theory and thus again suggests Wordsworth in his preoccupation with the poetic process of creation.

The initial situation in the creative process is, as already indicated, the prehension in which the concern of subject for object comes about through the function of object as provoker, thus causing in the receiving subject an affective tone or a concern that is conformal. Locke's concept of latent powers in things to attract, Whitehead refers to again and again; and this notion is one that Wordsworth must also have pondered.[18] But Locke was not concerned with metaphysical relationships as were Wordsworth and Whitehead. When the latter writes of objects in the actual world that they in abstraction ". . . are passive, but viewed in conjunction they carry the creativity which drives the world";[19] he goes a step beyond Locke. His concept of God as a non-temporal formative element in the creative process initiating appetition toward some constructive purpose through a lure for feeling, brings him closer to the pantheistic belief of Wordsworth that

> . . . the forms
> Of Nature have a passion in themselves,
> That intermingles with those works of man
> To which she summons him;[20]

and to the poet's recognition of

> . . . that universal power
> And fitness in the latent qualities
> And essences of things, by which the mind
> Is moved with feelings of delight,[21]

In calling attention to Locke's exposition of powers as "ascribed to particular existents whereby the constitution of other particulars are conditioned,"[22] Whitehead notes the use in the 19th century of the concept of the vector field as another illustration of the basic character of prehension and of the object to subject structure of experience. "Feelings," he said, "are vectors; for they feel what is *there* and transform it into what is *here*."[23] As a feeling, the positive prehension, an initial phase of creativity, reproduces in itself an external world to which it is referent and thus has a "vector character."[24]

Professor C. Clarke, a British scholar, in an article on Wordsworth's philosophy, calls his notion of "ever-during power" in the universe "energy conceived of poetically"— ". . . the positive and active quality of things by which they influence and dominate other things,"[25] and again suggests that though Whitehead was one hundred years and more in advance of Wordsworth and was further enlightened by the vector theory of physics, their ideas bore some resemblance.

The term prehension also includes the idea of appropriation which naturally follows attraction of object or datum for subject in the process of self-formation. The elements in the universe thus appropriated become ". . . components in the real internal constitution of [their] subject."[26] Thus ". . . every actual entity," Whitehead asserts, "has to house its actual world."[27] Then, ". . . the knowable is the complete nature of the knower. . . ."[28] Wordsworth's actual world during his great period was nature. "I had a world about me," he writes " 'twas my own";[29] and again

> . . . whate'er of Terror or of Love
> Or Beauty, Nature's daily face put on
> From transitory passion, unto this
> I was as sensitive as waters are
> To the sky's influence in a kindred mood of passion;[30]

Whitehead uses the term feeling to cover most phases of the concrescence of an actual occasion whether his emphasis is on attraction, positive prehension, appropriation, or perception; but to indicate that perception is something more than mere sensation he distinguishes two pure modes as presentational immediacy and causal efficacy.[31] In the first mode of perception he limits data to here and now; with senses alert one's impressions are vivid. Such perception is illustrated in The Prelude as Dorothy and William Wordsworth ". . . from some turret's head," are

Catching from tufts of grass and hare-bell flowers
Their faintest whisper to the passing breeze,
Given out while mid-day heat oppressed the plains.[32]

Presentational immediacy involves to a greater degree
than causal efficacy the "withness of the body." We see
with the eye, hear with the ears, touch with the hands—all
these organs being in themselves a part of nature. Indeed it
may be difficult at times to determine where our body ends
and the external world begins. Alexander indicates this
situation is due sometimes to the self overflowing in objects
one cares about, these then becoming an extension of his
body.[33] Lindbergh illustrates this notion in his feeling for
his plane, the *Spirit of St. Louis*, which he thought of at
times as a part of his body.[34] An instance of the functioning
of the body in experience is seen in Book I of *The Prelude*,
as perception of the world about the boy in the skating
episode is conditioned by his movements. Giving his body
to the wind appears to make it a part of nature and nature
a part of his own motion as he views it from here and now
with all his senses alert.

. . . and oftentimes,
When we had given our bodies to the wind,
And all the shadowy banks on either side
Came sweeping through the darkness, spinning still
The rapid line of motion, then at once
Have I, reclining back upon my heels,
Stopped short; yet still the solitary cliffs
Wheeled by me—even as if the earth had rolled
With visible motion her diurnal round![35]

Whitehead notes that ". . . the animal body is the great
central ground underlying all symbolic reference,"[36] the
interplay of the two pure modes of perception: presentational immediacy, just referred to, and causal efficacy, yet
to be discussed. The first, involving the senses in a prehension of the contemporary world is much more vivid, but to
Whitehead's mind, less significant than the second mode,

which is a more primitive feeling of a sense of inheritance from the world of the past. Our most primitive feelings, he says, are associated with the functioning of the body—common ground for both modes of perception. In the lowest grades of life causal efficacy, exemplified in feeling and action, is associated with an instinct for self-preservation; in the higher phases of experience it is seen in memory, which enters into our intuitional feelings. Like Whitehead, Wordsworth feels the ". . . force of obscure feelings representative of things forgotten,"[37] but his intuitions are more definitely mystical. In *The Prelude*, just before the poet had lost his way in crossing the Alps, his eagerness to continue is indicated.

For still we had hopes that pointed to the clouds,[38]

That yearning buttressed by memory, intuition, and imagination, illustrates causal efficacy embracing the future as well as the past, sharing with presentational immediacy the animal body when halted as it would carry out its aims, but rising superior to immediate sensation:

But to my conscious soul I now can say—
'I recognize thy glory': in such strength
Of usurpation, when the light of sense
Goes out, but with a flash that has revealed
The invisible world, doth greatness make abode,
There harbours; whether we be young or old,
Our destiny, our being's heart and home,
Is with infinitude, and only there;
With hope it is, hope that can never die,
Effort, and expectation, and desire,
And something evermore about to be.[39]

Both pure modes of perception have as common ground, not only the animal body but also the datum and ingredient eternal objects. But what has been perceived in the mode of causal efficacy as derived from the past and pointing toward the future, is enhanced or elucidated by perception in the mode of presentational immediacy. In the skating episode the recollection of the earth's "diurnal round" is intensified by the apparent motion of the shores of the lake. The interplay of these two modes Whitehead calls symbolic reference;[40] to this method of the transmission of feeling he gives great importance in his account of creative procedure. The interplay of percepta in both modes synthesized into one subjective feeling combines the immediate vivid realization of a particular scene with a general sense of existence in an awareness that is the highest phase of experience.

Wordsworth, just after crossing the Alps, illustrates this interplay between the two modes of perception. His direct view of the Alps shortly after they had lost their way is a magnificent example of symbolic reference. Omitting no detail of the picturesque region—a datum with ingredient eternal objects which serve with his animal body as a common ground for the interplay of percepta, he has a sense of life as it becomes and perishes, resolving its multiplicity of elements as symbols into the unity of eternal nature.

> . . . The immeasurable height
> Of woods decaying, never to be decayed,
> The stationary blasts of waterfalls,
> And in the narrow rent at every turn
> Winds thwarting winds, bewildered and forlorn,
> The torrents shooting from the clear blue sky,
> The rocks that muttered close upon our ears,
> Black, drizzling crags that spake by the way-side
> As if a voice were in them, the sick sight
> And giddy prospect of the raving stream,
> The unfettered clouds and regions of the Heavens,
> Tumult and peace, the darkness and the light—
> Were all like workings of one mind, the features
> Of the same face, blossoms upon one tree;
> Characters of the great Apocalypse,
> The types and symbols of Eternity,
> Of first and last, and midst, and without end.[41]

As process is for Whitehead the ultimate reality, it has been suggested that he does not give sufficient importance to mind.[42] True, he prefers to call it consciousness or mental operations, but mainly to avoid the traditional separation of mind and matter. In reviewing its place in his metaphysical system, one must see, however, that certainly in higher phases of experience it dominates the creative process. As subject it entertains appetitions or conceptual prehensions which Whitehead calls "the only operations of pure mentality."[43] Appetition develops into subjective aim which as controlling purpose determines to a large extent the outcome of process. Although for Whitehead the mind emerges from the world, that theory does not obscure the position of consciousness as the "crown of experience." To the mental pole of process or in higher phases of experience, consciousness, he also gives the important rôle of linking efficient and final causation.[44] He must have agreed to some extent with Wordsworth's assertion that the mind is "lord and master" and recognized in the poet's reasons for this supremacy his own convictions:

For, feeling has to him imparted power
That through the growing faculties of sense
Doth like an agent of the one great Mind
Create, creator and receiver both,[45]

But undoubtedly Wordsworth as well as Whitehead had derived from Plato the idea ". . . that being is the agent in action, and the recipient of action,"[46] such action probably referring to the antecedent actual world. Whitehead, however, notes also that the subject as recipient and agent is the vehicle of deity. As a pantheist, Wordsworth finds God in Nature and from Nature come to him that energy and calm receptivity that "constitute her strength."[47] God to Whitehead is that actual non-temporal entity from which each temporal concrescence or actual occasion receives the aim that starts its self-causation.[48] This lure for feeling or appetition is initiated by the eternal objects in the datum prehended in both modes of perception and included in

God's primordial nature. Wordsworth, for instance, in prehending the sunrise in Book IV of *The Prelude* feels positively the lure of glory and joy in the scene before him:
the mountains, the sea, the clouds, and the song of birds;
and the joy and glory as eternal objects permeate his own
soul, are intensified by contrasts, and result in an occasion
of experience expressed in his matchless description:

> . . . Magnificent
> The morning rose, in memorable pomp,
> Glorious as e'er I had beheld—in front,
> The sea lay laughing at a distance; near,
> The solid mountains shone, bright as the clouds,
> Grain-tinctured, drenched in empyrian light;
> And in the meadows and the lower grounds
> Was all the sweetness of a common dawn—
> Dews, vapours, and the melody of birds,
> And labourers going forth to till their fields.[49]

In the concrescence or growing together of the subject
and the related objects of this experience, the eternal objects thus have a double function: first in their ingression
into the elements positively prehended as a lure for feeling;
and secondly, in the admission of this lure in the affective
tone caught by the prehending subject from his original
concern for actual objects before him.

Neither Wordsworth nor Whitehead ever lose sight of
the fact that it is the blended might of mind and the external world that results in creation—that the lure for feeling (to Whitehead the germ of mind) imparts the power to
create through the "growing faculties of sense." During the
process of concrescence there is necessarily an interfusion
of mind and the world. Wordsworth calls it

> . . . an ennobling interchange
> Of action from without and from within;[50]

How is it possible, he questions, to

Run through the history and birth of each [sensation]
As of a single, independent thing.[51]

This query suggests Whitehead's repeated denial of the
definition of substance as something sufficient unto itself.
Because of inter-relationships, inter-connection, interfusion
he insists on the relativity of all elements in being.

This insistence is in keeping with his assertion that the
unit of actuality in life is process. Such an assertion, however, does not preclude the actuality of personal identity
which Whitehead designates as the historic route of actual
occasions. In this historic route he stresses the part played
by deity, "inscrutable workmanship," according to Wordsworth. Through reconciliation of contrasts a balance of
basic unity is achieved.

Dust as we are,

the poet writes,

> the immortal spirit grows
> Like harmony in music; there is a dark
> Inscrutable workmanship that reconciles
> Discordant elements, that makes them cling together
> In one society.[52]

To explain personal identity Whitehead uses an adaptation
of Plato's notion of "receptacle" as the "personal unity"
. . . "which receives all occasions of the man's existence. . . .
That which happens in it is conditioned by the compulsion
of its own past, and by the persuasion of its immanent
ideals."[53] This is as true of each event or actual occasion in
the historic route making up personality. Through the intervention of God comes that intensity of feeling aiming at
balance in the introduction of contrasts ". . . whereby the
indetermination of mere creativity [or process] is transmuted
into a determinate freedom."[54] Transmutation entering in
here as an enrichment of process through conscious percep-

tion is more significant in the creative advance of the world than mere transmission of feeling, which has been compared with action in the vector field of physics. Perception may arise indirectly through a combination of conceptual reversion and transmutation. Conceptual reversion brings novelty rather than mere reproduction; that is, conceptual feelings may be suggested to the subject by eternal objects inherent in data that are partly alike and partly different from the data of the subject's initial prehension, and then may be transmuted so as to be felt in the subject as if they were inherent in the original prehension.[55]

In Wordsworth's description of the sunrise, for instance, his original prehension may have been merely the glory of the sunrise over the mountains near at hand. The sea at a distance added the novel element of joy as it "lay laughing" —an element not incompatible with the glory of the bright clouds made radiant by the rising sun or the sweetness of fields and meadows with the melody of birds. Amid other elements seen that may have been eliminated from feeling by negative prehension and by subjective intensity, selection and evaluation emphasize the glory and the joy which, with the help of conceptual reversion and transmutation become the realized and balanced unity of the scene in what Whitehead calls "a determinate freedom" of creation.

During the achievement of this unity in which all elements of the concrescence are resolved in the final stage of the creative process[56] termed by Whitehead satisfaction, he notes the important part played by mind in the linking of efficient and final causation. Both efficient and final causes are clarified by his distinction between immanence and transcendence. Mental operations, Whitehead writes, make a ". . . decision derived from the actual world, which is the efficient cause" as well as a ". . . decision embodied in the subjective aim, which is the final cause."[57] Transcendence or potentiality is associated with the subjective aim; immanence or ingredience, with the actual world of the immortal past. "Concrescence [thus] moved toward its final cause, which is its subjective aim"; and "transition is the vehicle of the efficient cause, which is the immortal past."[58] With the completion of the process, wherein the old meets the new, comes satisfaction. The subjective aim having been attained, the actual occasion then perishes to remain in the guise of objective immortality or as an object exerting a lure for feeling on other subjects.

What Whitehead seems to mean by the linking of final and efficient causes in a definite creation of novelty may be better understood by applying his theories to a well-known passage in the latter part of Book XII in *The Prelude*. But first one must consider a somewhat parallel earlier passage, indicating an experience that results in a material satisfaction in which the final cause has little if any part.[59]

Noting Whitehead's interpretation of subject-object relation as that of recipient and provoker, we observe Wordsworth as a boy coming home for the Christmas holidays and waiting restlessly at the meeting of two roads for the horses that should bear him and his brothers to their home. On this day of wild and stormy weather he can see more clearly by climbing a mountain that rises up from the junction of the two highways. On one of these the horses must appear, and the boy watches eagerly, straining his eyes as the shifting mist discloses intermittently the roads and fields below. The violence of the storm continues, and close at hand within the boundaries of the boy's vision are an old stone wall, a single sheep, and a blasted hawthorne tree. All these elements of nature, in their fusion, suggest to him uncertainty, bleakness, and desolation, but these feelings are partially dismissed as in an "anxiety of hope" he awaits the fulfillment of his desire. Wordsworth does not dwell upon its satisfaction. It comes as an inheritance from the past when horses were provided for the boys' use rather than as a result of transcendental ideals that would give the experience objective value. The efficient cause only is active here in its transition from the past to the future or ". . . from attained actuality to actuality in attainment."[60]

How efficient and final causes may be linked in the satisfaction or final stage of an occasion will be seen in the passage following the event already given. The same scene brings to the poet future experience that has far more significance. He recounts his father's death during the Christmas holidays and his own grief. In a chastened spirit he repairs often again to the scene where he had looked and waited in "such anxiety of hope," seeing in his bereavement a divine correction of his desires. This sequence of events illustrates the historic route of occasions which build up, according to Whitehead, personality: a development in Wordsworth that resulted in some of the finest lines in *The Prelude*.

> And afterwards, the wind and sleety rain,
> And all the business of the elements,
> The single sheep, and the one blasted tree,
> And the bleak music from that old stone wall,
> The noise of wood and water, and the mist
> That on the line of each of those two roads
> Advanced in such indisputable shapes;
> All these were kindred spectacles and sounds
> To which I oft repaired, and thence would drink,
> As at a fountain;[61]

Now thoughts of eternal verities replace those of temporal pleasures, and he feels no longer the uncertainty and desolation identified with material things, but looks upon these elements of nature as enduring objects. The mist concealing the two roads but advancing "in such indisputable shapes" must have been as in a later phrasing of a similar scene

> . . . like an invitation into space
> Boundless, or guide into eternity[62]

Wordsworth's subjective aim now seems to be a quickening of the spirit. The lure for feeling comes as a thirst of his own spirit for the permanence and mystery of the spirit haunting nature. In the several features of the landscape he recognizes the eternal objects, harmony and endurance. There is an affirmative note in his mystic experience on the mountain top as the inspiration of these "kindred spectacles and sounds" reveals to him the spiritual unity of the whole. Thus he "thence would drink as at a fountain"; his thirst and the intensity of his subjective aim are satisfied.

The linking of associations of the past enduring into the present with the evocation of intensities as a result of Wordsworth's subjective and transcendent aim, brings here a completion of what Whitehead might term created value, through the working together of efficient and final causes. The efficient cause is the inheritance from the past: the familiar features of the landscape in the wind and rain and mist. The final cause identified with spirit in the primordial nature of God as well as in the external world, is the source of Wordsworth's lure for feeling, his poetic insight, and his mystic experience. From the blending of the old and the new, the efficient with the final cause, comes that quickening of the spirit toward which the poet was striving. The intensity of his transcendent aim has heightened the value of the living occasion. Recorded in lines of memorable poetry, it thus has not perished but remains to exert a lure for feeling on other subjects.

If Whitehead's interest in Wordsworth's *Prelude* was based largely on the poet's concern with the creative process, then the similarity in the approach of both to experience must have been due in part to their emphasis on the aesthetic. It is clear that Whitehead attaches great significance to the "aesthetic order of the universe" as he sees it.[63] In God's purpose, the evocation of intensities, he finds also the goal of art; for the evocation of intensities is an aesthetic experience—a feeling arising out of the realization of contrast under identity, and earlier expressed by Wordsworth as the perception of "dissimilitude in similitude."[64] "The actual world," Whitehead says, "is the outcome of the aesthetic order and the aesthetic order is derived from the immanence of God."[65]

Professor Bertram Morris notes Whitehead's important contribution to the analysis of the aesthetic situation whereby ". . . the process of art issues into beauty . . . ," citing his definition of beauty as "the mutual adaptation of the several factors in an occasion of experience."[66] He shows that the art process is essentially analogous to the various stages of process as Whitehead has analyzed them. Professor Stephen C. Pepper designates his own approach to the field of aesthetics as contextualism—a theory that shows much in common with Whitehead's metaphysics. "Fine art," Professor Pepper writes, "conscripts elements to function in the mutual determination of one another . . ." and he illustrates this statement by indicating the interweaving of strands or single processes in a texture or connected pattern of strands.[67] A parallel to these aesthetic theories in a description of beauty's birth through nature's interfusing energy has been noted by Professor Newton P. Stalknecht in Book XIV of *The Prelude*.[68]

> That mutual domination which she loves
> To exert upon the face of outward things
> So moulded, joined, abstracted, so endowed
> With interchangeable supremacy
> That men, least sensitive, see, hear, perceive
> And cannot choose but feel.[69]

Here Wordsworth in his meditation on Mt. Snowdon is concerned mainly with the poet's powers of creation, and reveals again a similarity to Whitehead in the creative process. Now the moon, supreme in the starry heaven, is a symbol of the poet's "majestic intellect,"

> . . . its acts
> And its possessions, and what it has and craves
> What in itself it is, and would become.[70]

Appropriation through prehension is suggested as well as appetition and process. The lure for feeling is powerful, for like the moon, the poet's mind "feeds upon infinity." It is

> . . . a mind sustained
> By recognitions of transcendent power,
> In sense conducting to ideal form,
> In soul of more than mortal privilege.[71]

In the poet's process of creating, the operations of soul and sense are linked by the mind's recognition of transcendent power, thus recalling immanence and transcendence in efficient and in final causation. The subjective aim fulfilled, objective immortality remains for the "soul of more than mortal privilege," an "immortality of realized value" as designated by Whitehead in his last word on the subject.[72]

Further quotations from *The Prelude* might be given to show the resemblance of Wordsworth's ideas on the creative process to the metaphysical theories of Whitehead—a resemblance in which the function of God in the world is particularly emphasized. But perhaps sufficient evidence has appeared to indicate that through the blended might of mind and the external world both poet and philosopher found creation possible: the mind deriving from God, and the material world exerting attraction through divine immanence.

VI

EPILOGUE

The lure for feeling we have seen to be a driving urge, a deep desire to achieve a goal; but this urge is not limited to higher phases of experience such as are involved in creative projects. Wherever a task is done superlatively well, this eternal urge has played its role, awakening latent powers. When Bob Turley of the New York Yankees won the Memorial Award as the major leagues' outstanding pitcher during the 1958 season, he was asked on television to what he attributed his success. He replied that it was mainly to a deeply felt desire for skill in delivering the ball. Skill in the pitcher's form of delivery has both traditional and contemporary value, and may be preceded by the same lure that leads man to accept as a task participation in the creative advance of the world. In such creative value, Professor Hocking sees "God at work in history"; and for him man's foresight and achievement spell God-given purpose to mankind.

Whitehead like Fechner would attribute purpose not only to man but in a sense to the entire natural world. To him there is no bifurcation of nature. Something approximating an unconscious purpose he sees in the lowest forms of life, in their reproduction and self-defence, in their battle for existence. Operations of mentality he conceives as "a diversion of the flow of energy," recognized also in what has commonly been called inanimate nature. Something that parallels an aim might be seen in the release or absorption of energy by electrons as they approach toward or retreat from the nucleus within the atom.

Purpose, which one associates with the lure, is engen-

dered by feeling; and here again is something deeply interfused throughout nature, a lure whose source is

A motion and a spirit, that impels
All thinking things, all objects of all thought,
And rolls through all things.

"It is the brooding presence of the hills" that haunts Wordsworth, Whitehead notes in *Science and the Modern World*
—a sense of solidarity in the changing forms of nature. In
the intermingling colors and forms of natural objects we
have found Whitehead also feeling a latent spirit of harmony and permanence.

In man the lure becomes an activating Eros entertaining ideas that may be relinquished or consummated in the
attainment of a goal, their use depending upon the possibility of their concrescence into a unified harmony. Conflicting ideas and situations delayed Lincoln in reaching
his goal with the Emancipation Proclamation toward the
end of the Civil War, but intensification of feeling in him
became a living urge. How to resolve conflicting issues of
North and South and save the Nation, preserve its basic
faith in freedom and equality? How to free the slaves in a
house divided against itself, now the South, now the North
gaining in the War? With malice toward none, with love
of God and of neighbor as his religious creed, Lincoln saw
in the gradual capitulation of the South ameliorating cir-
cumstances—a hope for the future of the country he loved
and for the preservation of its ideals. Only then could he
satisfy his deep desire to save the Union and abolish slavery.

God as the source of the lure for feeling may be clearly
felt in the experience of Lincoln; and this point of view
allies feeling with mysticism; but mystic feeling as revealed
in Whitehead cannot neglect facts—actual data. The objective world is so real to him that he hardly attempts to pierce
the veil beyond. Yet his faith is firm as is that of the poets
before him in the mystic influence of God in the world. He
suggests in fact that his philosophy of organism may be "a
transformation of some main doctrines of Absolute Idealism

onto a realistic basis"—so real that religion and science are fused "into one rational scheme of thought."[1] Before Whitehead, Emerson and Whitman had seen that the mystic and the scientist must become one.

Various examples from the contemporary world of philosophy and science might be given to show the power of feeling—the effects of intuition ending in novelty. Such effects in liberal arts studies disclose an inter-connection of subjects traditionally separated. It is the American democratic dream of freedom and equality, for instance, a political theory, that has infused novelty into our literature— fundamental ideals that are akin in the thinking of Lincoln, of Emerson, of Whitman, and of Mark Twain. Obscurities of scientific discoveries have been introduced to the layman through their suggestion in fiction; by as knowledgeable a person, for instance, as the English novelist, C. P. Snow.[2] World currents of thought, on the other hand, have led to novelty in the sciences—to the relativity of Einstein, and to the expanding atomic and quantum theories of Lord Rutherford and of Nils Bohr. In nuclear magic new wonders continually appear. God at work in history was apparent in the Christmas season of 1958 as there came from the giant satellite Atlas in outer space Eisenhower's message of peace and good will to all the world. The Kingdom of Heaven upon earth envisaged by Christ in his life time, Whitehead sees in his view of God's consequent nature—an embodiment of all values evolving from the lure—the driving urge of mankind seeking novelty that means value in the continual creative advance of the universe.

VII

GLOSSARY*

Abstraction has the usual meaning of withdrawal from the actual; but Whitehead stresses the point that complete abstraction would be self-contradictory since no entity can be considered as completely isolated. Abstraction may mean selection or elimination as an early step in process while the subjective aim points toward a novel entity. See *P.R.*, 42, 517.

Affective tone The occasion as subject in its concern for an object draws from it an affective tone that is as well directed toward it. The affective tone is in fact the subjective form or how of feeling in the successive prehensions of an occasion. See *A.I.*, 226, 315.

Appearance Reality and appearance form together the objective content of an occasion: the first, the data of the past, the world "from which the new occasion springs"; the second, the final data of the occasion reached through emphasis and combination in process. Whitehead calls appearance "a compound of reception and anticipation, which in its turn passes into the future." As a unit then it represents the goal of the lure for feeling. See *A.I.*, 268, 362, 355.

Appetition is an initial feeling of unrest in process that would realize "what is not and may be." Intensity of appetition evoked by God is needed to attain novelty and value; it is likened by Whitehead to vision. God's primordial

---

* Titles of the three books given mainly to the philosophy of organism are abbreviated in page references: *S.M.W.* for *Science and the Modern World*; *P.R.* for *Process and Reality*; and *A.I.* for *Adventures of Ideas*. References are to American editions.

appetition "is the basis of all order." See *P.R.*, 47, 48, 280, 323, 527.

Appropriation   Whitehead uses this term in explaining prehension—a subject's concern for an object to the end that he would make the datum his own. See *P.R.*, 249.

Causal efficacy can be best understood in contrast to *presentational immediacy*. Both are modes of perception: the first is dimly concerned with primitive experience and with the world in the past; the second is a more conscious, sophisticated regard of the contemporary world. The former in its suggestion of relatedness contributes to scientific theory; the latter in the sense of vivid and direct observation advances scientific knowledge. Linked with the responsive phase of process, causal efficacy comes closer to the lure for feeling. A part of the supplemental phase, presentational immediacy is felt in the individuality of decision or, as Whitehead suggests, in self-creation. See *P.R.*, 246, 184, 125, 257 & 273.

Comparative feelings comprise many sorts of complex feelings, but there are two simple types. 1) Unconscious physical purposes arising from the integration of initial physical prehensions with conceptual feelings suggested by the basic physical feelings. All actual entities, Whitehead claims, include a physical purpose. 2) Conscious intellectual feelings derived only in part from the initial physical phase. Intellectual feelings include propositional feelings that arise from the physical feelings from which they are partly derived; and these as affirmative or negative in their subjective forms are conscious. See *P.R.*, 249 & 406.

Conceptual reversion   As a phase of conceptual feeling, conceptual reversion originates with prehension of data "partially identical with and partially diverse from eternal objects in data of the primary phase of the subject's mental pole." A unified determination of identity and diversity depends on the depth of intensity in the subjective aim by reason of contrast. "The contrasts produced by reversion," Whitehead claims, are "contrasts required for the fulfillment of the aesthetic ideal." See *P.R.*, 40, 380 & 390.

Concern as perception is the basic subject-object relation in experience. Concern is the term used for the feeling of an occasion as subject for an object. This feeling parallels the positive prehension of datum. See *A.I.*, 226 & 232.

Conformal feelings belong to the initial responsive stage of process. This Whitehead calls also the individualizing phase; here the subject conforms to its object—the datum or data—by reproducing what is felt in the how of feeling or in the subjective form. Through perspective the initial data become the objective datum. See *S.M.W.*, 102.

Concrescence means growing together, the coming of many into one. For such concrescence all entities have potentiality. Through concrescence of feelings selected and emphasized by the subjective aim of an occasion the entity becomes itself. "Concrescence moves towards its final cause, which is its subjective aim." Actuality is participation in concrescence. See *A.I.*, 303 and *P.R.*, 33, 232, 320 & 321.

Consciousness arises with the integration of conceptual and physical feelings, is provoked by an abstract element in a concrete fact, is felt in negative perception, in the contrast of negative and affirmative, and in recognizing the difference between what is and what may be. It is the crown of experience, requiring recollection and thus following earlier and more primitive phases of feeling which remain a part of a higher phase. Since pure conceptual feelings are devoid of consciousness, God in his primordial nature is infinite and unconscious; in his consequent nature he is finite and conscious. See *P.R.*, 371, 370, 245, 372, 408, 246, 521 & 524.

Consequent nature of God This is the incarnation of the world in God. His derivative nature is consequent upon the creative advance of the world and integrates with the primordial nature of God, being "determined, incomplete, consequent, everlasting, fully actual and conscious." Whitehead emphasizes patience as a part of his consequent nature in taking care that nothing be lost. The wisdom of God's subjective aim as He prehends organic actualities is seen in his judgment on the world. In the objectification of the world in God, everlastingness is identified with objective immortality. See *P.R.*, 524, 525 & 527.

Creativity is the principle of novelty, the ultimate behind all forms, but it is conditioned by God. The factor of activity in the initial situation of an occasion is creativity. "Objects viewed in conjunction carry the activity that drives the world." In terms of contrasted opposites God and World, "creativity achieves its supreme task." See *P.R.*, 31, 528; *A.I.*, 230, 231.

Efficient cause The relation of an occasion to other earlier occasions objectified in the actual world constitutes its efficient causation. The inflow of the actual world is the efficient cause as it participates in the concrescence of an occasion; tradition and environment are of help in explaining efficient causation. See *P.R.*, 134, 374 & 159.

Entity Actual occasions and eternal objects are the two most important types of entities. Generally speaking an entity means "potentiality for process," and that includes God; but the decision of an entity in process adds the force of actuality. Eternal objects are pure potentials and not actual. The metaphysical character of an entity Whitehead indicates as being "a determinant in the becoming of actualities." See *P.R.*, 68, 392.

Eternal objects are derived from Plato's universals, and are envisaged by God in all their multiplicity; but are not as in Plato a hierarchy ending in the Good. God is not a universal; nor are eternal objects archetypes to be copied on earth. As exemplified in a color they may be recognized conceptually without reference to any actual entity; but in actual entities their potentiality is realized. See *Propositions*. The metaphysical status of an eternal object is being a possibility for an actuality. See *S.M.W.*, 229, and Chapter X, *passim.*

Event In *Science and the Modern World* the event is associated with relativity—a fundamental principle with Whitehead. It is called a space-time unity with a past, present, and future. An occasion is a limiting type of event, which usually, like a nexus, has inter-related occasions; for example, an historic route making up personality. See *S.M.W.*, 106 and *P.R.*, 113 and 174.

Feelings The two main types of feeling are physical and conceptual; they are allied with the physical and mental poles of a subject. A physical or causal feeling has for its datum another entity; a conceptual feeling, an eternal object. The former type of feeling is prior to the latter. Whitehead calls conceptual feelings operations of pure mentality, in which case they are unconscious. All complex feelings arise from the integration of conceptual and physical feelings. The basic conceptual aim is derived from God, in whose primordial nature all eternal objects are envisaged. See *P.R.*, 365, 366, 49, 343.

Final cause This is the end toward which the occasion aims in its becoming. This subjective aim or purpose, if the goal is value, like all such desire, is grounded in the primordial nature of God, and emerges as the lure for feeling. In the functioning of the final cause, novelty is introduced— an element absent from inherited data. Efficient and final causes may be united by decision concerned with the actual world and by decision involved with the subjective aim. See *P.R.*, 159 & 423.

God It is because Whitehead makes God a supreme example of an actual entity, and because process is more important to Whitehead than fact that creativity rather than God is his ultimate. In God's primordial and consequent natures there are the mental and physical poles of a living occasion. In Whitehead's early discussion of an underlying eternal energy, he would seem to have both creativity and God in mind, for he speaks of the envisagement of eternal objects and of the possibilities of value as well as of the actual entities participating in process. All this is as close to God, the principle of concretion, as to creativity, the principle of novelty. In *Process and Reality* Whitehead reaches the highest point in his interpretation of God. His purpose is depth of satisfaction in human experience. From Him the basic conceptual aim of each temporal entity is derived. Without his intervention there would be nothing new and no order in the world. In his consequent nature are love, judgment, and patience. God in his function of the kingdom of heaven is seen in "the multiplicity of actual components in process of creation." See *S.M.W.*, 154 f. and *P.R.*, 343, 525, 531.

Immanence means first of all the presence of God in the world; this makes belief in pure chaos impossible. Immanence also makes for the unity of nature and the unity of each human life. It is the "past energizing in the present." The future is also immanent in the present in a special sense. Immanence in process and in eternal objects is understood best by contrasting it with transcendence. Immanence is involved in the formal consideration of an actual entity— of the process within it during its becoming. The transcendence of the process is its objective aspect—the potentialities which the subject aims to realize. Immanent decision is the determinant in process. Immanence describes an eternal object that has been actualized; transcendence indicates its capacity for determination. See *P.R.*, 169; *A.I.*, 241 and 247; *P.R.*, 336 and 367.

Infinite is a term rarely applied to the deity by Whitehead. It has rather the meaning Plato gives to it in the *Philebus*, of the many entities in the world varying in their degrees of qualification. Whitehead applies it to an abstractive hierarchy of eternal objects that do not stop "at a finite grade of complexity." See *S.M.W.*, 242.

Intensity, Whitehead says, issues from harmony in contrasts—contrasts that may be felt between realized eternal objects. The creative emphasis of each occasion is "in proportion to its measure of subjective intensity." God's purpose, Whitehead affirms, is intensity of experience. The evocation of intensity comes from Him through the lure. See *P.R.*, 167, 75 & 161.

Interfusion Whitehead uses this term for the final notion with which, according to the poets, a philosophy of nature must be concerned. This idea of inter-connection means to him that a substance is not sufficient unto itself. The necessary inter-dependence of things "he finds presupposed by the Laws of Nature." See *S.M.W.*, 127, 155, 156.

Internal Relations, Doctrine of Togetherness, which Whitehead stresses in the actuality of process, means the inter-connections of entities in the concrescence of a new occasion. In this process there are two factors governing internal relations: the subjective aim and form; and the various related components of the concrescence that are unified by "individualized activity." Examples of internal relations are the interconnection of mental and physical functions, of the past with the present, and the immanence of the cause in the effect. See *S.M.W.*, 180 and *A.I.*, 201.

Lure Whitehead designates a proposition as a lure for feeling—the lure of a theory seeking truth. The lure may also be the final cause, the subjective aim, and the germ of mind. The main role of an eternal object is that of a conceptual lure for feeling. At all times the lure is associated with the idea of potentiality. As the eternal urge of desire, God assumes the function of the lure. See *P.R.*, 37, 281, 130 & 522.

Metaphysics Whitehead's metaphysical position is that "the understanding of actuality requires a reference to ideality." The metaphysical standpoint he calls "a dispassionate consideration of the nature of things." Metaphysics, he believes to be an essential background for science and even for civilization. See *S.M.W.*, 228 & 227. *A.I.*, 164.

Mind The germ of mind Whitehead sees in the lure. Mind is also implied in the complex of mental operations involved in the concrescence of an occasion. Mental operations need not be fully conscious, but are so in the case of affirmative or negative judgments or when recollection is a factor. Whitehead prefers the term *mental operations* as it does not suggest separation of body and mind. See *P.R.*, 130, 326.

Mutual immanence Whitehead sees exemplified in Plato's receptacle—a medium of intercommunication. There is mutual immanence in a family of occasions in a society or nexus. Any such set of occasions has unity through their mutual immanence. See *A.I.*, 172, 258 & 254. See *Interfusion* and *Internal relations*.

Negative prehension is the elimination from feeling or the exclusion of items from a positive contribution to an occasion. A negative prehension, however, indicates definite emotional experience of the subjective form. The feeling, Whitehead says, "retains the impress of what it might have been, but is not." See *P.R.*, 35, 66 & 346.

Nexus is one of four notions diverging from thought of earlier philosophy. It is a public matter of fact in expressing the togetherness of actual entities. The nexus, Whitehead says, may be formally complete like an event as process ends in satisfaction, or it may be objectified as the actual world of an actual entity. For this entity in process, its initial data is multiplicity, which in perspective becomes an objective datum or nexus. See *P.R.*, 27, 32, 124 & 338.

Novelty Creativity is the principle of novelty, and God as the organ of limited novelty conditions creativity. "In virtue of its novelty," Whitehead claims, "every actual entity transcends its universe." Conceptual novelty originates in life as a bid for freedom beyond the scope of tradition. This is seen as process follows the category of conceptual reversion. (See definition) Novelty entertained by the subject may meet the objective datum from the past and thus create value in the combining of new and old. Contrasting elements enter essentially into novelty. Like aesthetic experience, it arises out of the realization of contrast under identity. Novelty may be good or bad, but as value is finally embodied in the consequent nature of God. See *P.R.*, 31, 164, 143, 159, 427 & 525.

Object All things as potentials for feeling may be objects. An object provokes the concern of the subject of an occasion; and in object to subject structure there is the relation of cause to effect. Entities are objectified by the mediation of eternal objects that are factors in their definiteness, showing a transcendent element toward which the occasion in question aims. The goal may be complex developing through successive prehensions, which Whitehead calls causal bonds. See *P.R.*, 89; *A.I.*, 226; *P.R.*, 361, 230.

Objective immortality Occasions ending in value perish after becoming as occasions. They remain, however, in objective immortality, as stubborn facts enduring through their novelty and value in the consequent nature of God— his incarnation in the universe. See *P.R.*, Part V.

Occasion The world is built up of actual occasions which are also actual entities and were originally termed

events. The name event is later ascribed to a family of
occasions or a nexus. The occasion is a concresence in process consisting of prehensions from mental and physical
poles of subject. Every occasion has a subject, an object, a
subjective aim, form, and satisfaction. With satisfaction it
becomes and then perishes. See *P.R.*, 113, 124 & 32.

Ontological Principle This is one of Whitehead's four
notions diverging from earlier philosophic thought. In his
words "every condition to which the process of becoming
conforms in any particular instance has its reason either in
the character of some actual entity in the actual world of
that concrescence or in the subject which is in the process
of concrescence." According to the ontological principle the
reason for any actual entity may be found in some other
actual entity; it is the principle of efficient and final causation, the ultimate basis of the final cause being the conceptual valuation of eternal objects by God in his primordial
nature. See *P.R.*, 27, 36 & 392.

Organism Whitehead calls the universe "in any stage
of its expansion" an organism. An organism is a concrete
fact in its actual becoming. It is the actual occasion in
process of concrescence. Thus the idea of an organism must
include that of the interaction of organisms. See *P.R.*, 327
and *S.M.W.*, 55 & 151.

Perception Prehensions, Whitehead indicates, do part
of the work for perception, but he is careful to explain that
perception in which only the sense organs are concerned
has a limited meaning. He would add non-sensuous elements in which recollection has a part. Two kinds of perception he distinguishes sharply: that of causal efficacy
and that of presentational immediacy. See definitions of these
two. Their interplay in symbolic reference plays a large part
in human experience. See *S.M.W.*, 104; *A.I.*, 229, 231; and
P.R., 274, 275.

Personal order ". . . an *enduring object,* or *enduring creature,* is a society whose social order has taken the special
form of *personal order.*" A thread of personal order is seen
along some historic route of members in a society. This

means that a definite type of hybrid prehensions has been "transmitted from occasion to occasion of its existence." See definition of *prehension*. Such transmission may result in an enduring personality. See *P.R.*, 50, 163 & 182.

Poles—physical and mental "Each actuality is bi-polar: physical and mental"; and mentality is "a reaction from and integration with, physical experience. . . ." The physical and mental poles are contrasted aspects of the creative urge: the first having its source in causal or physical feeling; the second, in conceptual feeling; thus "the mental pole originates as the conceptual counterpart of operations in the physical pole." The subjective side of experience comes from the mental pole; the objective side, from the physical pole. See *P.R.*, 165, 366, 379 & 423.

Prehension is called in *Science and the Modern World* "uncognitive apprehension" or perception of objects within the unity of mind. In its response to and reproduction of an external world the prehension has a vector character; it has three factors: subject, datum, and subjective form; it is physical or conceptual, not involving consciousness in either case. Physical and conceptual prehensions when combined are impure or hybrid. A positive prehension is a feeling meaning transmission from the objectified data to the concrescence of the prehending subject. A negative prehension eliminates from feeling. In a prehension the affective tone of concern is always present. See *S.M.W.*, 101; *P.R.*, 35; and *A.I.*, 232.

Presentational immediacy See *causal efficacy*.

Primordial Nature of God In this primordial nature, God envisages the entire realm of eternal objects or potentials in their relevance to basic conditions of creativity. As pure conceptual feelings are devoid of consciousness, He in his abstract function is unconscious and actually deficient, though infinite, free, complete, and eternal. Through his consequent nature he becomes fully actual and conscious. As He in his primordial nature determines the relevance of eternal objects for each creature, he is called the principle of concretion. In his action upon the world through his conceptual feeling he is also "the lure for feeling, the eternal urge of desire." His aim is "a depth of satisfaction as an intermediate step toward the fulfillment of his own being." See *P.R.*, 521, 134, 524, 522 & 161.

Private Immediacy, Whitehead calls the self-functioning of the actual entity in process. It is understood best in reference to feelings which at first are merely responsive, but in the privacy of experience, what was re-enaction or second-handedness becomes first-handedness as in Whitehead's phrasing, repetition is *overwhelmed* by immediately felt satisfaction. With the completion of the occasion immediacy perishes. The importance of understanding the immediate occasion in its relation to past and future is emphasized in *Science and the Modern World*. See *P.R.*, 38, 234, 206, 130 and *S.M.W.*, 64.

Process That "being is constituted by its becoming is the principle of process." It is a becoming that ends in concrete fact as many become one. This interaction of elements is essential to the expansion of the universe to which the term *process* may also be applied. "Actuality [is] in its essence a process." See *P.R.*, 35, 65, 327 and *A.I.*, 355.

Proposition A proposition is a theory that functions as a lure for feeling—a lure seeking truth. As an entity it means potentiality for process; but in this respect it differs from an eternal object in that it is true or false and "grounded upon reason." A reason, Whitehead claims, always has reference to some actual entity, but an eternal object may be conceived without any such reference. The proposition in process is akin to what Whitehead calls a physical purpose. It is an integration of the initial feeling with the conceptual feeling it suggests, expressed in the form of a theory. Ex. A prehension of life awakening in the spring by Wordsworth from his garden seat, suggests a conceptual feeling of joy and leads to the proposition: All animate life in the spring suggests joy. See *P.R.*, 281, 392, 342.

Propositional feelings come under comparative feelings, their datum a proposition. The proposition's relation to the actual world through its subjects make it a lure—like an eternal object potential, indeterminate. The propositional feeling is not essentially conscious; it is an intermediate between the purely physical stage of feeling and intellectual feelings. But as the subject integrates propositional feelings with other feelings consciousness may arise in subjective forms. See *P.R.*, 249, 391, 395, 393.

Reality   In Whitehead's use of *reality* and *actuality*, the former term is generally applied to the objectification of entities. In process "the potential unity of many may acquire the real unity of one"; and this means objectification. The future, Whitehead calls merely real, because it may be objectified conceptually in the present; but it is not actual. In speaking of a proposition as realized when admitted into feeling, he means objectified for feeling. The actual world appropriated with its own realized form objectified, may be a datum for feeling. "The kingdom of heaven," Whitehead finds, "is with us today," in objective immortality, for "what is done in the world is transformed into a reality in heaven"—in the consequent nature of God. "And the reality in heaven then passes back into the world." See *P.R.*, 33, 327 & 532.

Re-enaction   Whitehead calls reproduction or conformation in process as he refers to subject and datum. Re-enaction may also mean reiteration when the word signifies something more than endurance and is akin to vibration in physics. A simple physical feeling is the partial reproduction of its cause's feeling, that of the datum. It means a two-way functioning of an eternal object that determines in part the objective data and in part the subjective form. Re-enaction continues in successive prehensions as they become more complex through contrasts; and with the force of repetition, intensity arises. The rhythmic character of experience allied with repetition or vibration adds stability as well. See *S.M.W.*, 193; *P.R.*, 364, 426.

Relativity   "Essential connectedness," Whitehead says, "is the doctrine of thoroughgoing relativity." It is the idea of an entity as a factor in the process of becoming, and of actual entities as present in others. The reason that an event does not move is the internal character of all its relatedness. If it were not for intensive relevance entities might be "undifferentiated repetitions." See *A.I.*, 197; *P.R.*, 78; *S.M.W.*, 180; and *P.R.*, 224.

Relevance is akin to *relatedness* with the added sense of *bearing upon:* for instance the relevance of the immediate past to the present. Two statements in the philosophy of organism support a doctrine of relevance between a form and any occasion of which it is a part: 1) God is the basic completeness of appetition; 2) each occasion including God effects a concrescence of the universe. The canalization of relevance from the primordial nature of God accounts for originality. "The *relevance* of an eternal object in its rôle of lure is a fact inherent in the data." See *P.R.*, 481, 164 & 131.

Satisfaction is the final phase in the process of concrescence. Therefore the subject as a component in the concrescence is not conscious of the satisfaction. It is, however, a complex definite feeling unifying all elements in the concrescence. It gives individuality and concreteness to the entity in question—is an outcome apart from the process while the actuality of an entity includes process as well as outcome. The unity of feeling called satisfaction "embodies what the actual entity is beyond itself. It is two-dimensional: its narrowness and width representing intensity and coordination. See *P.R.*, 38, 129, 335 & 252.

Society is a nexus with a social order—where "there is a common element of form illustrated in the definiteness of each included entity." Societies may be corpuscular or non-corpuscular. Examples: 1) when concerned with occupied space; 2) when concerned with wider physical field in empty space. There is a hierarchy of wider and wider societies, Whitehead notes, from the society of molecules to the geometric society of this cosmic epoch. There is no absolute gap between living and non-living societies. The orderly element in an environment may be seen in its societies. See *P.R.*, 50, 112, 293, 148, 156 & 169.

Soul In *Science and the Modern World*, the term does not appear. In *Process and Reality*, Hume's use of soul and mind, Whitehead says, is analogous to his actual entity or occasion; here he stresses the fusion of soul and body. As human occasions succeed each other, personal identity evolves and this is called the soul of man. For further clarity he refers to Psyche and Eros from whom he found Plato deriving his later notions of life and motion. The mental side of process Whitehead identifies with Plato's Eros—a soul enjoying its creative function, arising from its entertainment of ideas. As mind emerges from the world, its correlate, the soul, evolves from mental and physical experiences. See *P.R.*, 213; and *A.I.*, 243, 355 & 189. *N.L.*, 40.

Subjective aim This in occasions as a force Whitehead sees "governing the whole tone of human life." It is both the aim and the goal of an occasion—the lure and the final cause. The subjective forms or how of feeling originate in the subjective aim that is thus a unifying factor in process. In the evolving of the subjective aim in process, spontaneity is an important regulative principle. The aim unites the efficient and the final cause by linking the decision from data in the actual world with decision from the conceptual aim derived from God. See *P.R.*, 74, 343; *A.I.*, 328; and *P.R.*, 423.

Subjective form is partly due to the qualitative element in data prehended from the actual world; but it is more than a reproduction or repetition of feeling. As the how of feeling it is a private matter of fact arising from the subjective aim. This how of feeling develops through different stages of process or successive prehensions and becomes consciousness in higher phases of experience, acquiring intensity in development. Negative prehensions may enter into the subjective form. Spontaneity of feeling is important in governing the unity of the subjective form. See *P.R.*, 246, 247, 32; and *A.I.*, 325, 328.

Subject As a feeler, the subject is one of three factors in every prehension; the other two are the datum or object and the subjective form or how of feeling. The objects or object bear a causal relation; the subject is the effect. All actual things, Whitehead finds, are alike subjects and objects; that is, all entities may pass beyond themselves in their interaction with other entities; and all entities have the power to intervene in the development of other entities. The subject emerges from the occasion a superject. The subject's function is involved with the privacy of feeling; the superject, having become, endures as a public fact. See *P.R.*, 35, 361, 89 & 443.

Superject An entity is at once a subject and a subject superject toward which it aims. The subject through its subjective aim experiences in privacy its own creation as final superject. This is achieved when through unified feeling satisfaction is attained. The occasion then loses its actuality but endures as superject in objective immortality to be considered henceforth in reference to the publicity of things. Whitehead calls it "a moment of passage from decided public facts to a novel public fact." See *P.R.*, 43, 108 and 443.

Symbolic reference is the interplay between two types of perception: causal efficacy and presentational immediacy; and as in all symbolism there must be a common ground between the two correlates. The "great central ground underlying all symbolic reference," Whitehead names as, "the animal body." This in its functioning is best known through causal efficacy; in its appeal to the senses, through presentational immediacy; but the earlier experience, according to Whitehead, is that of causal efficacy. "We are subject to our percepta," he says, "in the mode of causal efficacy; we adjust our percepta in the mode of presentational immediacy." See *causal efficacy*. See *P.R.*, 258, 267 & 271.

Transition is flux or fluency exemplified in concrescence as process moves toward its final cause. Transition also carries on the efficient cause—the immortal past—into the concrescence of a new living occasion. Because of transition, which is closely allied with creativity, the world never really is, for any relatively complete actual world is a potential datum for a new occasion. Whitehead calls transition "one all-pervasive fact"—a passage requiring time and space and not limited to a linear progression. See *P.R.*, 320, 322 and *S.M.W.*, 135.

Transmuted feeling follows physical and conceptual feeling. In none of these phases is consciousness of necessity involved, but it is more likely in transmuted feeling. Here one physical feeling in a final subject may be derived from various similar physical feelings entertained by various members of a nexus together with their various similar derivative conceptual feelings. The similarity consists in the fact that the physical and conceptual feelings of each member of the nexus exhibit the same ingredient eternal object. This object then serves as a private element in subjective form and as an agent in objectification, for the final subject sees this eternal object to be definitive of the nexus as one. Let the nexus be an orchestra with many members playing respectively different instruments. The eternal object *precision* derived from the physical response of a subject to the performance of a drummer, is felt by the same subject in the playing of the other members of the orchestra. The character of precision by transmutation is then applied to the orchestra as one. See *P.R.*, 40, 355, 362, 384 & 446.

Value   The subjective aim of an occasion is naturally novelty or value in the final satisfaction. As novelty, however, may be good or bad, the two are not quite synonymous. The emergence of value in the concrescence of an occasion necessitates limitation, which is derived in part from God's primordial valuation of eternal objects in their relevance to actual entities. Conceptual reaction to such eternal objects introduces purpose, which is qualified by an intermediate phase of self-formation in process. With adversion or aversion, valuation up or down, comes limitation, the outcome of the subjective aim in satisfaction and value. See *P.R.*, 164, 368 & 388.

Valuation is the subjective form of conceptual feeling that "introduces creative purpose." This valuation is a common factor in occasions; for conceptual feeling is derived from physical feeling through valuation. It may take the place of consciousness in propositional feelings. The source of valuation is seen in the primordial nature of God, who envisages the relevance of all pure potentials to his creatures, and thus conditions creativity. See *P.R.*, 380, 402 & 374.

Vector character "All things," Whitehead says, "are vectors." In nature the vector structure appears as the immanence of the past energizing in the present. Prehensions have a vector character in transferring feeling from data or objects to the subject of the occasion—cause thus passing into effect. The vector form characterizing flux or actuality is submerged as entities attain satisfaction and objective immortality. See *P.R.*, 471; *A.I.*, 241; and *P.R.*, 323.

NOTES

In my discussion of the lure for feeling, the Macmillan Company has kindly allowed me the use of quotations from Whitehead's three main texts on the philosophy of organism. These are *Science and the Modern World, Process and Reality,* and *Adventures of Ideas,* whose copyright dates are respectively 1925, 1929, and 1933. Macmillan also permits me to use brief quotations from *Religion in the Making* (Copyright, 1926) and from *Nature and Life* (Copyright, 1934). Permission to use quotations from *The Philosophy of Alfred North Whitehead* (Copyright, 1941 by Library of Living Philosophers, Inc.) and edited by Paul A. Schilpp, has been given by Professor Schilpp. I am indebted to the Houghton Mifflin Company for numerous quotations from the Centenary edition of Emerson's *Works,* from his *Journals,* and from the *Writings* of John Burroughs. Acknowledgment should also be given to Alfred A. Knopf, Inc. for permission to use lines from Chinese poetry in their translations by Arthur Waley (Copyright, 1919) and by Witter Bynner (Copyright, 1929).

References to the following works of Whitehead will be cited as given below:

C. N. for *The Concept of Nature* (Cambridge University Press, 1920). Courtesy of publisher.

S.M.W. for *Science and the Modern World* (New York, 7th reprint, 1931).

R.M. for *Religion in the Making* (New York, 1926).

N.L. for *Nature and Life* (The University of Chicago Press, 1934).

P.R. for *Process and Reality* (New York, 3rd reprint, 1941).

A.I. for *Adventure of Ideas* (New York, 13th printing, 1952).

Chapters and sections listed will help in using English editions.

Sections rather than pages are given in references to Goethe's works as the edition used by Emerson is not easily available.

Microfilm for Emerson's unpublished journals are available at the Columbia University Library and at the Houghton Library at Harvard.

Notes—Preface

1. Among studies that have already indicated an interest of Emerson in Goethe's natural philosophy are the following: F. B. Wahr, *Emerson and Goethe* (Anne Arbor, Mich., 1915); P. R. Sakmann, "Ralph Waldo Emerson's Goethebilde." *Jahrbuch der Goethe Gesellschaft,* XIV (1928), 166-190; F. B. Wahr, "Emerson and the Germans," *Monatshefte für Deutschen Unterricht,* XXXIII (1941), 49-63; and K. W. Cameron: Emerson's *Nature* (1836) ed. in Scholars' Facsimiles and Reprints (New York, 1940) and *Emerson the Essayist* (Raleigh, N. C., 1945).

2. Platonic influence in general has been carefully treated in *Whitehead's Philosophy of Organism* by Dorothy M. Emmet (London, 1932).

3. "Science and Man's Freedom," *Atlantic Monthly* (Sept., 1957) Vol. 201, No. 9, pp. 73, 74.

4. Cited in "Mechanistic Biology and the Religious Consciousness" by Joseph Needham in *Science, Religion and Reality* ed. by Needham (New York, 1925), 251.

Notes—Chapter I

1. *The New York Times* (Sunday, May 30, 1937).

2. It is well known that Wordsworth's pantheistic nature poems were written mainly in his golden decade (1798-1808), that in 1814 he denied the influence of Spinoza in his

poetry, and that in 1850, when he published *The Prelude,* many of his pantheistic passages were revised. In his greatest nature poetry, however, the pantheistic element still stands.

3. The similarity of Wordsworth's attitude to that of the Chinese has been indicated by various students of Chinese philosophy and art. Among these are Irving Babbitt in *Rousseau and Romanticism* (Boston, 1919), 395; Shigeyoshi Obata, translator of *The Works of Li Po, The Chinese Poet* (New York, 1928), 19; Witter Bynner, translator of *T'ang shih san pai shou, The Jade Mountain* (New York, 1929), xvii; and Laurence Binyon in *Landscape in English Art and Poetry* (London, 1931), 145.

4. Investigation of possible sources for the pantheistic and mystical elements underlying Wordsworth's great nature poetry might lead back through Schelling and other German romantic writers, Spinoza, Boehme, Bruno, Erigena, and Dionysius the Areopagite, to Plotinus and the Stoics. See W. R. Inge, *Christian Mysticism* (London, 1933, 7th ed.) and N. P. Stalknecht, *Strange Seas of Thought* (Duke University, N. C., 1945). Coleridge's early interest in the dynamic philosophy of nature (*Biographia Literaria,* Chapter IX) was probably shared by Wordsworth.

5. Ch'an Buddhism is better known to the West by the Japanese name of Zen.

6. Fung Yu-lan, "The Philosophy of Chu Hsi," translated by Derk Bodde, *Harvard Journal of Asiatic Studies,* VII (April, 1942), 1-23. Complete translation by D. Bodde of *A History of Chinese Philosophy* by Fung Yu-lan, in 2 vols. (Princeton University, 1952, 1953).

7. "The Works of Mencius," Book VII, chapter IV, *The Chinese Classics,* Vol. I, translated by James Legge (London, 1861), 326. This represents the belief of Chu Hsi.

8. J. P. Bruce, translator of *The Philosophy of Human Nature* by Chu Hsi (London, 1922), 180, 183.

9. "The Recluse" (London, 1891), Book I, 1.52.

10. W. E. Hocking, "Chu Hsi's Theory of Knowledge," *Harvard Journal of Asiatic Studies,* I (1936), 124.

11. *The Prelude,* Book XIII, 11. 8-10.

12. Hocking, loc. cit., 124.

13. A. N. Whitehead, *Science and the Modern World* (New York, 1931), *S.M.W.,* 122. Chapter V.

14. See last lines of Book XIII in *The Prelude* for Wordsworth's conception of "spiritual dignity."

15. See F. S. C. Northrop, *The Meeting of East and West* (New York, 1947), 315 ff. See also O. J. Campbell, "Wordsworth's Conception of the Esthetic Experience," *Wordsworth and Coleridge;* studies in honor of George McLean Harper. Ed. by Earl Leslie Griggs (Princeton, 1939), 26-47.

16. Strictly speaking neither the term *pantheist* or *mystic* is completely applicable to the Chinese writers or to Wordsworth since the Supreme Power in the universe was to them transcendent but not the only reality. See *Encyclopedia of Religion and Ethics,* IX (New York, 1922), 65, 612. The term *panentheism* has been used by Inge, *op. cit.,* and by others for belief in the immanence of a God who is also transcendent.

17. *The Prelude,* Book VI, 11.606-608.

18. See Derk Bodde, "The Chinese view of immortality: its expression by Chu Hsi and its relationship to Buddhist thought," *Review of Religion,* VI (1932), 369-383.

19. The date of the *Tao Te Ching* is controversial because of the uncertain date of its presumable author. The book may have been written in the sixth century B.C., and at least was known by Chuang Tzu, who lived in the fourth and third centuries B.C.

20. Arthur Waley, *The Way and its Power* (Boston, 1935, 2nd ed.) (By courtesy of Houghton Mifflin Co.)

21. "Lines Composed a Few Miles Above Tintern Abbey," 11.95-101.

22. Waley, *op. cit.,* 170.

23. *Ibid.,* 58.

24. "Expostulation and Reply."

25. Waley, *op. cit.,* 162.

26. Campbell, *op. cit.*

27. *Chuang Tzu, Mystic, Moralist, and Social Reformer,* translated by Herbert Giles. (Second Edition Revised (Shanghai, 1926), 279, 280.

28. *Ibid.,* "The Great Supreme," 89.

29. *The Prelude,* Book XIV, 11. 188-192 and 130-132. See Stalknecht, *op. cit.,* Chap. VI. Mr. Stalknecht believes that *intellectual love,* as used here, was definitely influenced by that of Spinoza in his conception of the third mode of knowledge.

30. From *170 Chinese Poems* by Arthur Waley (By permission of Alfred A. Knopf, Inc., copyright 1919 by Alfred A. Knopf, New York, 6th printing, 1938), 100.

31. *The Prelude,* Book VI, 11.742-744.

32. Hu Shih, "Development of Zen Buddhism in China," *Chinese Social and Political Science Review,* XV (January, 1932), 483.

33. D. T. Suzuki, *Essays in Zen Buddhism,* First Series (London, 1927), 231.

34. Arthur Waley, "Chinese Philosophy of Art," II, *Burlington Magazine,* XXXVIII (London, 1921), 32.

35. Letter of Nov., 1811, in W. A. Knight, *Memorials of Coleorton,* II (Boston, 1887), 152.

36. See Martha Hale Shackford, *Wordsworth's Interest in Painters and Pictures* (Wellesley, 1945), 32, 33.

37. John Ruskin, *Works,* III (London, 1903), 177, 178. Note particularly in *The Prelude,* Book VIII, 11.77-97, a description of a Chinese landscape. The accurate details of characteristic features suggest that Wordsworth had seen some landscape paintings from China.

38. Because Chu Hsi was chiefly responsible for the creation of the Neo-Confucian system, I have used Chu Hsi's and Neo-Confucian theories synonymously when referring to this philosophy. Chu Hsi did have important predecessors, however, whose ideas he incorporated in his system of thought. Fung Yu-lan, *op. cit.,* 10.

39. *Ibid.,* 18.

40. Ibid., 10. See *The Book of Changes, Sacred Books of the East,* Vol. 16, translated by Legge (Oxford, 2nd ed., 1899).

41. Fung Yu-lan, "The Rise of Neo-Confucianism and its Borrowings from Buddhism and Taoism," translated by Derk Bodde, *Harvard Journal of Asiatic Studies,* VII (July, 1942), 90. See Note 6.

42. Fung Yu-lan, "The Philosophy of Chu Hsi," Translator's introduction, 6.

43. See Note 4 for possible sources of Wordsworth's dynamic philosophy of nature.

44. Chapter I, 4, *The Chinese Classics* translated by James Legge, I (London, 1861), 248.

45. Chapter X, 4, *The Chinese Classics,* I, 238.

46. Chapter XX, 18, 19, *The Chinese Classics,* I, 277.

47. Fung Yu-lan, "The Rise of Neo-Confucianism," 106.

48. *Ibid.,* III, 112.

49. The Prelude, Book XIV, 1.71.

50. *The Tao of Painting* by Mai-mai Sze. Bollingen Series XLIX, Bollingen Foundation, Inc. (New York, 1956), Vol. II, 24.

51. "The Doctrine of the Mean," Chapter XXVI, 1-5, *The Chinese Classics,* I, 28.

52. Book IX, 11.3-15.

53. Leibnitz found Chu Hsi's philosophy in harmony with his dynamic theory of the universe. See Henri Bernard, S.J., "Chu Hsi's Philosophy and its Interpretation by Leibnitz," *T'ien Hsia Monthly* (Shanghai, 1937), 18.

54. A. Waley, "Chinese Philosophy of Art," I, *Burlington Magazine,* XXXVII, 309.

55. *The Prelude,* Book IV, II.319-332.

56. Laurence Binyon, *Painting in the Far East* (London, 1908), 137.

57. Raymond Havens, *The Mind of a Poet* (Baltimore, 1941), Chapter IV.

58. Willard L. Sperry, *Wordsworth's Anti-Climax,* Harvard Studies in English, XIII (Cambridge, 1935), 197.

59. *The Prelude,* Book XII, 11.317-326.

60. From *The Jade Mountain* by Witter Bynner, 144.

61. *The Prose Poetry of Su Tang-p'o* translated by Cyril D. Le Gros Clark (Shanghai, 1935), 22.

62. Osvald Sirén, *The Chinese on the Art of Painting*

(Peking, 1936), 66. This was in accord with the first and most important rule for Chinese painting, *ch'i yun,* originating with Hsieh Ho in the 5th century. His principle has been translated "spirit resonance" (Sirén, *op. cit.,* 19, 21). Courtesy of author.

63. *Ibid.,* 51. Sirén speaks of the artist's profound tranquility or emptiness of mind before identification with his object as preparation for painting was possible.

64. *Lankāvatāra Sutra* A Mahayana Text translated by D. T. Suzuki (London, 1932), 294.

65. Sirén, *op. cit.,* 107.

66. Lines 348-352.

67. Olin Downes cited earlier. See also Laurence Binyon, *The Flight of the Dragon* (London, 1911), 19.

68. Lucy Driscoll and Kengi Toda, *Chinese Calligraphy* (Chicago, 1936).

69. Fung Yu-lan, "The Philosophy of Chu Hsi," 23.

70. See Sirén, *op. cit.,* 97; and also Okakura Kakuzo, "Taoism and Zennism," *The Book of Tea* (Sydney, Australia, 1935), 29. See also Mahayana doctrine of void, above.

71. Osvald Sirén, *A History of Early Chinese Painting* (London, 1933), II, 135, 136. Courtesy of author.

72. *The Spirit of Man in Asian Art* (Cambridge, Mass., 1935), 101. The painting may be seen at the Boston Museum of Art and is entitled "Bare Willows and Distant Mountains."

73. Sirén, *A History of Early Chinese Painting,* II, 24.

74. Florence Ayscough, *Tu Fu,* II (London, 1934), 294. (By courtesy of Jonathan Cape, Limited.)

75. *Ibid.,* II, 306.

76. Witter Bynner, *op. cit.,* 114.

77. Shigeyoshi Obata, Translator, *The Works of Li Po* (New York, 1928), 144. (By courtesy of E. P. Dutton and Company, Inc.)

78. Book VIII, 11.266-286.

79. Obata, *op. cit.,* 71.

80. Arthur Waley, "Chinese Philosophy of Art," IV, *Burlington Magazine,* XXXVIII (London, 1921), 244. Mr.

Waley quotes from *The Great Message of Forests and Streams* based on writing of Kuo Hsi and composed by his son Kuo Ssu.

81. *Ibid.*

82. *The Prelude*, Book VI, 11.604-605.

83. Osvald Sirén, *A History of Early Chinese Painting*, II, Plates 94, 95, 96. This scroll may be seen in the Boston Museum of Art and is called "Clear Weather in the Valley."

84. *Ibid.*, II, 92, 95.

85. *Ibid.*, Plate 54.

86. "Lines Composed a Few Miles above Tintern Abbey."

87. *The Prelude*, Book VIII, 11.567-569.

88. Obata, *op. cit.*, 40.

89. Sirén, *A History of Early Chinese Painting*, II, "An Angler on a Wintry Lake" by Ma Yüan, Plate 59. See also Bynner, *op. cit.*, "An Old Fisherman" by Liu Tsung-yuan (773-819), 99.

90. Sirén, *ibid.*, I, 95. See also Arthur O. Lovejoy, *The Great Chain of Being: A Study of the History of an Idea* (Cambridge, Mass.: Harvard University Press, 1936), 303-304. The author speaks of the German romantic writers as thinking that "the artist's task is to imitate, not simply Nature's works, but her ways of working." This is the essence of the organic theory followed by Goethe, Wordsworth, Whitman, and others.

91. Sirén, *ibid.*, II, Plate 55.

92. *The Tao of Painting*, II, 101. See note 50.

93. "The Doctrine of the Mean," Chapter XXXI, 2, 3, *The Chinese Classics*, I, 292, 293.

94. Book XIV, 11.39-40 and 70-77.

95. No attention has been given in this study to the steadily increasing awareness in Europe of Chinese art and culture from the fourteenth century up to the time of Wordsworth, for this development points to no real evidence of Chinese influence in his thinking.

NOTES—CHAPTER II

1. *The Prelude*, Book II, 11.28, 29.
2. D. W. Gotschalk. *Metaphysics in Modern Times* (Chicago, 1940), 70 ff.
3. *Types of Philosophy* (New York, 1929), 372.
4. *P.R.*, 11. Part I, Chapter I, Section II.
5. *Philosophy in a New Key* (Mentor Book, N. Y., 4th printing, 1952), 236.
6. *S.M.W.*, 154, 157, 158. Chapter VI.
7. *P.R.*, 50, 524. Part I, Chapter III, Section I; Part V, Chapter II, Section III.
8. *Ibid.*, 47. Part I, Chapter III, Section I.
9. *S.M.W.*, 228. Chapter X.
10. *P.R.*, 522. Part V, Chapter II, Section II. This point will be discussed further in Chapter III, Section on Immanence.
11. *Ibid.*, 126. Part II, Chapter II, Section VI.
12. *S.M.W.*, 48. Chapter II.
13. *Ibid.*, 70. Chapter III.
14. See "Whitehead's Philosophical Development," in *The Philosophy of Alfred North Whitehead*, ed. P. A. Schilpp (New York, 2nd ed., 1951), 33-46.
15. *A.I.*, 216. Chapter X, Section IV.
16. *P.R.*, 63. Part II, Chapter I, Section I.
17. *Ibid.*, 28. Part I, Chapter II, Section I.
18. *Ibid.*, 481. Part IV, Chapter IV, Section II.
19. *A.I.*, 230, 231. Chapter XI, Section 10.
20. See *P.R.*, 399, Part III, Chapter IV, Section III.
21. *Ibid.*, 408. Part III, Chapter V, Section II.
22. *R.M.*, 104.
23. *A.I.*, 319. Chapter XVI, Section VII.
24. *Ibid.*, 355. Chapter XIX, Section II.
25. *P.R.*, 531. Part V, Chapter II, Section VI.
26. *A.I.*, 381. Chapter XX, Section XI.

Notes—Chapter III

1. P.R. Sakmann, "Ralph Waldo Emerson's *Goethebilde*," *Jahrbuch der Goethe Gesellschaft*, XIV (1928), 166-190.

2. Letter to Covers Francis, April 24, 1837, *The Letters of Ralph Waldo Emerson*, ed. R.L. Rusk (New York, 1939), II, 72. Courtesy, Columbia University Press and Emerson Memorial Association.

3. "Plato; New Readings," Centenary Edition of *The Complete Works of Ralph Waldo Emerson*, ed. E. W. Emerson (Boston, 1883-1904), IV, 85. Emerson's edition of Goethe's *Werke: Vollständige Ausgabe letzter Hand . . . Stuttgart und Tübingen:* J. G. Cotta, 1827-1833. In 1836 Emerson bought the 15 posthumous volumes.

4. Letter of Emerson to Grimm, Jan. 5, 1871, *Correspondence between Ralph Waldo Emerson and Herman Grimm*, ed. F. W. Hollis (Boston and New York, 1903), 85. Noted by R. L. Rusk in *op. cit.*, I, lii.

5. Ms. C R, 1871, pp. 3, 4. Houghton Library, Harvard College.

6. "Works and Days," *Works*, VII, 170.

7. A.I., 166, Chapter VIII, Section VI.

8. Ms. 214.108, Houghton Library.

9. From *"Eins und Alles"* of *"Gott und Welt"* in *Werke* III, *op. cit.*

10. "The Method of Nature," *Works*, I, 197; III, 196.

11. *P.R.*, 63, Part II, Chapter I, Section I.

12. *Journals of Ralph Waldo Emerson* ed. E. W. Emerson and W. E. Forbes 1864-1876 (Boston, 1909-1914), I, 359 (Mar. 21, 1824).

13. *Goethe as Scientist*, translated by Heinz Norden (Abelard-Schuman Limited. Copyright, 1949, N. Y.), 233.

14. "Seashore," *Works*, IX, 243; "The Man of Letters," *Works*, X, 249, 250.

15. "Fate," *Works*, VI, 31.

16. "Powers and Laws of Thought," *Works*, XII, 16. From 1848, when this lecture was first given in England,

Emerson gave much attention to the relation between mind and matter; and transcendentalism gave way to objective idealism as noted by S. B. Whicher in *Freedom and Fate* (University of Penna. Press, 1953) and by P. Sherman, *Emerson's Angle of Vision* (Harvard University Press, 1952).

17. Letter to John Heath, Aug. 4, 1846. Rusk, *op. cit.*, III, 77. See note 2.

18. *P.R.*, Preface, vi.

19. *Journals*, VIII, 507. (Oct. 11, 1854.)

20. *P.R.*, 35. Part I, Chapter II, Section II.

21. For Whitehead, see *S.M.W.*, 154 ff. Chapter VI.

22. "The Scholar," *Works*, X, 276, 277.

23. *Journals*, II, 118 (Sept. 23, 1826).

24. "Instinct and Inspiration," *Works*, XII, 71.

25. "Powers and Laws of Thought," *Works*, XII, p. 40.

26. G. Schaeder, *Gott und Welt* (Hameln, 1947), 150. Quoted from letter to Schiller, 6.1-1798.

27. *Emerson's Angle of Vision* (Harvard University Press, 1952), 222.

28. "Powers and Laws of Thought," *Works*, XII, 51, 58.

29. *Literary History of the United States*, ed. R. E. Spiller, W. Thorp, T. Johnson, H. S. Canby (New York, 1948), 353.

30. V. Lowe, "The Development of Whitehead's Philosophy" in Schilpp, *op. cit.*, 76, 78.

31. *Wilhelm Meister's Wanderjahre, Werke*, XXI, XXII, XXIII, *Kunst, Ethisches, Natur. "In den Werken des Menschen wie in denen der Natur sind eigentlich die Absichten vorzüglich der Aufmerksamkeit wert.*

32. Paul, *op. cit.*, 209.

33. E. Neff. *The Poetry of History* (New York, 1947), 65.

34. *A.I.*, 305. Chapter XIV, Section XVII.

35. *Werke*, XLVII, *Aus Kunst und Altertum*.

36. F. W. G. Schelling, *Von der Welt Seele* (1798). See *Werke*, II (Stuttgart, 1857), 342.

37. *S.M.W.*, 127. Chapter V.

38. "Instinct and Inspiration," *Works*, XII, 74.

39. *Ibid.*

40. *P.R.*, 35. Part I, Chapter II, Section II.

41. Unpublished Journals G L, 1861-63. Microfilm at Columbia University Library. See also "The Sovereignty of Ethics," *Works* X, 183.

42. *A.I.*, 99. Chapter V, Section III.

43. *P.R.*, 319. Part II, Chapter X, Section I; *A.I.*, 171, Chapter VIII, Section VII.

44. *Journals*, IX, 31 (April 5, 1956). Unpublished Journals, S O, 1856. Microfilm, C U L.

45. *P.R.*, 522, 523. Part V, Chapter II, Section II.

46. *Ibid.*, 47. Part I, Chapter III, Section I.

47. Unpublished Journals—1842 and Ms. 214.108, Houghton Library.

48. Ms. 214.108, Houghton Library.

49. In J. P. Eckermann, *Gespräche mit Goethe* (Leipzig, 1937), II, 200; this Emerson was reading in April, 1837. See *Journals*, IV, 218. Cf. also Sarah Austin, translater of Falk's *Characteristics of Goethe* (London, 1833), 267-78; this read by Emerson. Spinoza was on Emerson's reading lists for 1837 and 1838.

50. See R. B. Luce, "A Comparative Study of Certain Basic Categories in the philosophies of Leibniz and Whitehead" (Unpublished dissertation, Dept. of Philosophy, Harvard University, 1940).

51. See letter from Aunt Mary, *Journals*, X, 138 (February, 1866) and "Immortality," *Works, VIII*, 338.

52. *Types of Philosophy*, 107.

53. The *Epirrhema* and *Antepirrhema* in Greek comedy are both called recitatives following the *Parabase*, which is an address of the chorus or leader of the chorus to the audience in the name of the poet.

54. See "Worship," *Works*, VI, 240.

55. This essay, not published until 1878, dates back in material to a lecture on morals in 1859. In *Journals*, IX, 251 (Oct., 1859) Emerson speaks of God as "constituting the health and conservation of the universe." Cf. *Journals*, VI, 219; *Works* X, 199.

56. Schilpp, *op. cit.*, 674.

57. "The Poet," *Works*, IX, 322. Saadi and Hafiz are both mentioned here, but in Unpublished Journals (X, 1845), lines quoted are identified with Hafiz.

58. Schaeder, *op. cit.*, 150.

59. *Vortrag gehalten in Königsberg*, 1853 in pamphlet ed. by W. König, 1917, p. 18.

60. Ms. 214.116, Ms. 214.119, Houghton Library.

61. *P.R.*, 182. Part II, Chapter IV, Section V.

62. *N.L.*, 46.

63. "Walter Savage Landor," *Works*, XII, 348; "Compensation," II, 97; "Progress of Culture," VIII, 224.

64. "Instinct and Inspiration," *Works*, XII, 82.

65. *Op. cit.*, 219.

66. *Werke, L, Polarität*.

67. See *N.L.*, 37; *A.I.*, 50.

68. *R.M.*, 105.

69. *C.N.*, 142.

70. "Clubs," *Works*, VII, 239.

71. "Progress of Culture," *Works*, VIII, 223, 232.

72. Cf. F. I. Carpenter, *Emerson and Asia* (Harvard University Press, 1930), 74, 75, Chapters III & IV, *passim*.

73. K. P. Hasse, *Von Plotin zu Goethe* (Leipzig, 1901), 311.

74. "The Poet," *Works*, IX, 311.

75. *N.L.*, 28-38. Part II.

76. See *P.R.*, 177. Part II, Chapter IV, Section IV; *N.L.*, 46.

77. "Compensation," *Works*, II, 124.

78. *Journals*, VIII, 528 (Feb., 1855).

79. *Werke, L., Über Naturwissenschaft im Allgemeinen*.

80. See W. C. Peebles, "Swedenborg's Influence upon Goethe," *Germanic Review* (July, 1933), Vol. VIII, No. 3.

81. Unpublished Journals, V O, 1857. Microfilm.

82. *P.R.*, 528. Part V, Chapter II, Section IV.

83. *S.M.W.*, 154, 155. Chapter VI.

84. *R.M.*, 92.

85. *P.R.*, 249. Part II, Chapter VII, Section V.

86. *A.I.*, 230, 231. Part III, Chapter XI, Section 10.

87. "Quotation and Originality," *Works*, VIII, 200. *Jour-*

nals, II, 349 (Oct., 1830). No source given. Cf. *Characteristics of Goethe,* Falk Von Miller, *op. cit.,* III, 76, 77. Letter from Goethe to Pierre Dumont of June, 1830.

88. See R. P. Adams, "Emerson and the Organic Metaphor," *P M L A,* LXIX (March, 1954), 117-130.

89. "Mathematics and the Good," Schilpp, 679.

90a. Rusk, II, 246 (Dec. 23, 1839); *Works,* I, 210; *Works,* XII, 42.

90b. *P.R.,* 161. Part II, Chapter III, Section X.

91. Ms. 214.108, p. 14. Houghton Library, See V. C. Hopkins, "The Influence of Goethe on Emerson's Aesthetic Theory," *Philological Quarterly,* XXVII (Oct., 1948); also her *Spires of Form* (Harvard University Press, 1950).

92. *P.R.,* 63, *loc. cit.,* "The Method of Nature," *Works,* I, 198.

93. *S.M.W.,* Chapter V, 135.

94. Cf. S. Lawrence, *Whitehead's Philosophical Development* (University of California, 1956), 257.

95. *Werke, L, Naturwissenschaft. "Die Natur hat sich soviel Freiheit vorbehalten dass wir mit Wissen und Wissenschaft ihr nicht durchgängig beikommen oder sie in die Enge treiben können.*

96. "Love," *Works,* II, 180.

97. "Illusions," *Works,* IX, 288.

98. Ms. 200.2, "Relations of Intellect to Natural Science," II, 52. Houghton Material.

99. *Journals,* X, 457, 462 (From Ledgers of uncertain date, 1862-1872).

100. (New York, 1958), 163.

101. *Op. cit.,* 96.

NOTES—CHAPTER IV

1. *Dictionary of American Biography.*

2. See C. Barrus, *Whitman and Burroughs, Comrades* (Boston, 1931).

3. *S.M.W.,* Chapter I, 23.

4. *Ibid.*

5. L. Price, *Dialogues of Alfred North Whitehead* (Bos-

ton, 1954), 22. Courtesy of Little, Brown, and Co. and of Atlantic Monthly Press.

6. *Writings of John Burroughs* (Boston, 1871-1922), XXI, 213.

7. *Ibid.*, XVIII, 260.

8. See R. Bucke, *Cosmic Consciousness* (New York, 6th ed., 1929), 215-237; *World Bible,* ed. by R. O. Ballou (New York, 1944), 56; W. E. Hocking, *The Coming World Civilization* (New York, 1957), 31, 32.

9. *Writings,* XX, 229.

10. *Ibid.,* XXI, 324.

11. *Ibid.,* XIII, 267.

12. Preface of 1855, *Leaves of Grass* ed. by E. Holloway (New York, 1924), 493.

13. *Walt Whitman Hand Book* (Packard and Company, Chicago, 1946), 246.

14. *Writings,* XIX, 223.

15. *Ibid.,* XVI, 193.

16. "Song of the Universal."

17. *S.M.W.*, Chapter XII, 274.

18. *Writings,* XXIII, 38.

19. *Ibid.,* XXI, 56.

20. *Ibid.,* XIII, 234-35.

21. *Ibid.,* XVIII, 179.

22 *A.I.*, 375. Chapter XX, Section VII.

23. *Writings,* XIV, 259; XXI, 109, 110.

24. *R.M.*, 104, 105.

25. L. Price, *op. cit.,* 22.

26. Preface to 1855 Edition, Holloway, *op. cit.,* 504.

27. "A Backward Glance," *Ibid.,* 534.

28. "Song of the universal."

29. "A Backward Glance," Holloway, *op. cit.,* 534.

30. *R.M.*, 160.

31. *Writings,* XXIII, 234; XIV, 179.

32. *Ibid.,* XVII, 87. See also *A.I.*, 147. Chapter VII, Section VI.

33. *Ibid.,* XXIII, 52.

34. *Ibid.,* XIX, 231.

35. *S.M.W.*, Chapter XII, 275.

36. See J. E. Miller Jr., *A Critical Guide to Leaves of Grass* (University of Chicago Press, 1957), 82, 88.

37. *S.M.W.*, Chapter V, 123, 125.

38. *Works*, II, 139.

39. *N.L.*, Part II, 40.

40. *Writings*, XV, 220; XVIII, 50.

41. *Ibid.*, XXIII, 2.

42. *Ibid.*, XVIII, 285.

43. *A.I.*, See 248, 249. Chapter XII, Section I. See *P.R.*, 75.

44. *Writings*, VIII, 49.

45. See *P.R.*, 40, 41 and 323. Part I, Chapter II, Section III; Part II, Chapter X, Section III.

46. *Writings*, X, 31.

47. *Ibid.*, XVI, 203.

48. *A.I.*, 35, Chapter III, Section I.

49. Note interfusion is used as one of the six notions demanded by the poets in a philosophy of nature, *S.M.W.*, Chapter V, 127.

50. *Writings*, X, 136.

51. *Ibid.*, XVIII, 265.

52. *Ibid.*, XXI, 64.

53. *Ibid.*, XIII, 221.

54. *Ibid.*, XIV, 253.

55. *A.I.*, 144. Chapter VII, Section V.

56. *Writings*, XXI, 29.

57. Cf. *Writings*, XIII, 217.

58. Sections 44 and 51.

59. "Song of Myself," Section 46.

60. *Writings*, XIII, 235.

61. *S.M.W.*, Chapter VI, 154 ff.

62. *A.I.*, 237-39. Chapter XI, Sections 16 and 17; See also *P.R.*, 177-79. Part II, Chapter IV, Section IV. See *S.M.W.*, Chapter VI, 145.

63. *P.R.*, 29, Part I, Chapter II, Section I.

64. See George W. Gray, *The New World Picture* (Boston, 1936), 301.

65. *Writings*, I, xv.

66. *Ibid.*, XIII, 233.

67. *Ibid.*, XVII, v.
68. *Ibid.*, VIII, 254.
69. *Ibid.*, XV, 61.
70. 1847 Note-book quoted by Allen, *op. cit.*, 259.
71. Allen, *op. cit.*, 410, Note 64.
72. *Writings*, XVI, 162.
73. "Laws for Creation."
74. *Writings*, III, 216.
75. *Ibid.*, XXI, 324, 325.
76. See Miller, *op. cit.*, Chapter XVIII.
77. *Writings*, XVI, 261.
78. *Ibid.*, XIII, 248.
79. *Ibid.*, XVIII, 270.
80. "Song of Myself," Section 46.
81. *Writings*, XVIII, 273, 274.
82. Sections, 46, 44 and 20 in "Song of Myself."
83. *N.L.*, 40.
84. *The Coming World Civilization*, 198.

<h2 style="text-align:center">Notes—Chapter V</h2>

1. V. Lowe, "The Philosophy of Whitehead," *Antioch Review* (Summer, 1948) and "Whitehead's Philosophical Development," Schilpp, *op. cit.*, 118.

2. *Dialogues of Alfred North Whitehead* as recorded by L. Price, *op. cit.*, 195, 369; *S.M.W.*, 126. Chapter V.

3. "The Recluse," Passage from conclusion used as Preface of 1814 ed. of *Excursion*.

4. "The Philosophical Aspects of the Principle of Relativity," *Proceedings of Aristotelian Society, New Series,* XXII (London, 1922), 216.

5. Information given by Miss Jessie Whitehead, November, 1953.

6. See Lowe, in Schilpp, *op. cit.*, 98; A. N. Whitehead, *R.M.*, 90-93; and Charles Hartshorne, "Whitehead's Idea of God," in Schilpp, 526, 527.

7. *P.R.*, 408. Part III, Chapter V, Section II.

8. *Ibid.*, 224. Part II, Chapter VI, Section III. Cf. *S.M.W.*, 228e.s. Chapter X.

9. *P.R.*, 113. Part II, Chapter II, Section IV.

10. *A.I.*, 226. Chapter XI, Section 3.

11. *P.R.*, 374. Part III, Chapter III, Section I. Cf. also *S.M.W.*, 136, Chapter V and 257, Chapter XI.

12. *P.R.*, 130. Part II, Chapter III, Section I.

13. *The Prelude*, XIV, 1.71 and 1.112. "Such minds are truly from the Deity." As Whitehead's family believe he never saw Selincourt's work on the manuscripts of *The Prelude*, quotations are taken from the 1850 version.

14. "The Recluse," passage already cited, 11. 69-72.

15. This is the substance of a remark made to Professor Victor Lowe and kindly reported to me.

16. *P.R.*, 317-326. Part II, Chapter X, Sections I through IV.

17. *A.I.*, 227. Chapter XI, Section 5.

18. See S. G. Dunn, "A Note on Wordsworth's Metaphysical System," *English Association Essays and Studies*, XVIII (Oxford, 1932), 75, 76. See also Coleridge, *Biographia Literaria*, Chapter IX.

19. *A.I.*, 230, 231. Chapter XI, Section 10.

20. *The Prelude*, XIII, 11. 291-294. See Whitehead's comment on Wordsworth's theme: "nature *in solido*," *S.M.W.*, 121, 122. Chapter V.

21. *The Prelude*, II, 11. 324-327.

22. *P.R.*, 222. Part II, Chapter VI, Section II.

23. *Ibid.*, 133. Part II, Chapter III, Section I.

24. *Ibid.*, 28. Part I, Chapter II, Section I.

25. "Nature's Education of Man—Some Remarks on the Philosophy of Wordsworth," *Philosophy*, XXIII (London, 1948), 303. *See Excursion*, IV, last part.

26. *P.R.*, 353. Part III, Chapter I, Section X.

27. *Ibid.*, 124. Part II, Chapter II, Section VI.

28. *Ibid.*, 92. Part II, Chapter I, Section VII.

29. *The Prelude*, III, 1. 141.

30. *Ibid.*, 11. 133-141.

31. *P.R.*, 179-192. Part II, Chapter IV, Sections V-IX. Cf. *A.I.*, Chapter XIV.

32. *The Prelude*, VI, 11. 221-223.

33. *Space, Time and Deity*, I (London, 1927), 106.

34. *The Spirit of St. Louis* (New York, 1953), 228, 292.

35. *The Prelude*, I, II. 452-460.

36. *P.R.*, 258. Part II, Chapter VIII, Section I.

37. *The Prelude*, 11. 605-607.

38. *Ibid.*, 1. 587.

39. *Ibid.*, 1. 598-608.

40. *P.R.*, 255-279. Part II, Chapter VIII. Cf. his discussion of appearance in *A.I.*, 344, 348. Chapter XVIII, Sections III and V.

41. *The Prelude*, VI, 11. 624-640.

42. See R. W. Sellars on substance and W. E. Hocking on mind in Schilpp, *op. cit.*, 429, 400.

43. *P.R.*, 49. Part I, Chapter III, Section I. Cf. *A.I.*, 270. Chapter XIV, Section II.

44. *P.R.*, 423. Part III, Chapter V, Section VII. Cf. *A.I.*, 272. Chapter XIV, Section IV.

45. *The Prelude*, II, 11. 255-258.

46. *A.I.*, 154. Chapter VIII, Section II.

47. *The Prelude*, XIII, 11. 1-10.

48. *P.R.*, 343. Part III, Chapter I, Section V. Cf. *S.M.W.*, 257. Chapter XI.

49. Lines 323-332.

50. *The Prelude*, XIII, 11. 376, 377.

51. *Ibid.*, II, 226, 227.

52. *Ibid.*, I, 11. 340-344.

53. *A.I.*, 240, 241. Chapter XI, Section 19.

54. *R.M.*, 90.

55. *P.R.*, 40, Part I, Chapter II, Section III; 410, Part III, Chapter V, Section IV.

56. Professor Clarke notes that Wordsworth believed in the creative principle in all things—the power which creates unity out of a given multiplicity. *Op. cit.*, *Philosophy*, 1948, 304.

57. *P.R.*, 423. Part III, Chapter V, Section VII.

58. *Ibid.*, 320. Part II, Chapter X, Section I.

59. Lines 287-305.

60. *P.R.*, 326. Part II, Chapter X, Section V.

61. *The Prelude*, XII, 11. 317-326. See here also an

example of Wordsworth's theme as noted by Whitehead:
"nature *in solido*."

62. *The Prelude,* XIII, 11. 151, 152.

63. See B. Morris, "The Art Process and the Aesthetic
Fact in Whitehead's Philosophy," Schilpp, *op. cit.,* 463-486.

64. See *Preface to Lyrical Ballads,* 1800.

65. *R.M.,* 105.

66. Morris, *op. cit.,* 465; *A.I.,* 324. Chapter XVII, Section I.

67. Courtesy of S. C. Pepper, *Aesthetic Quality* (N. Y.,
1937), 11, 32.

68. N. P. Stalknecht, "Nature and Imagination in Wordsworth's Meditation upon Mt. Snowdon," *P M L A,* Vol. 52B
(N. Y., 1937), 838.

69. Lines 81-86.

70. Lines 67-69.

71. Lines 74-77.

72. "Immortality," Schilpp, *op. cit.,* 688.

EPILOGUE—NOTES

1. *P.R.,* VIII, Preface.

2. See *The Search* (N. Y. and London, 1958).

INDEX

F

Faraday, M., 75, 79.
Fechner, G. T., 51, 148.
Feeling, 28, 36, 135, 142.
Final Cause, 26, 35, 39, 49, 63, 66, 122, 142, 145; see also subjective aim and purpose.
Foerster, N., 104.

G

God, 2, 3, 33, 41, 51, 130. See also principle of concretion and of limitation.
God, consequent nature of, 22, 24, 26, 42, 50, 60, 61, 70, 88, 108, 150.
God, primordial nature of, 22, 24, 26, 29, 42, 53, 67, 70, 88, 98, 108, 145.
Goethe, XI, XII, XIII, Chapters III and IV, *passim.* See references to "*Gott und Welt,*" 43, 50, 53, 59, 61, 63, 65, 66, 68, 81, 86, 93, 100, 123; and to *Italienische Reise,* 47, 57, 59, 71, 85, 91, 94.
Gottschalk, D. W., 24.

H

Hafiz, 71, 72, 80.
Havens, R., 11.
Helmholtz, G., 44, 73.
Herder, J. G., 49, 59, 72, 85, 86.
Hocking, W. E., XIV, 2, 25, 67, 103, 105, 128, 148.

I

Idealism, 43, 45, 51, 64, 111, 149, 150.
Immanence, 33, 34, 35, 47, 52, 61-69, 96, 111, 112-115, 145.
Immortality, 3, 112.
Intensity, 28, 37, 38, 39, 53, 68, 77, 79, 82, 87, 93, 94, 118, 125, 132, 145.
Interfusion, 52, 88, 78-87, 118-121.
Internal relations, doctrine of, 119. See mutual immanence.

J

James, W., 53, 129.
Jesus of Nazareth (Christ), 34, 41.

K

Kant, 64.
Kingdom of Heaven, 34, 41, 112, 150.
Kuo Hsi, 14, 17.

L

Lamarck, 73, 105, 108, 116.
Langer, S., 26.
Lao Tzu, 4.
Leibnitz, 33, 46, 49, 50, 59, 66, 74.
Lilienthal, O., 24, 35.
Lincoln 149.
Li Po, 15, 16, 18.
Locke, 129, 134.
Lowe, V., XIV, 33, 130.
Lure for feeling, XI, XII, 22, 24, 27, 28, 38, 39, 41, 54, 55, 64, 78, 82, 87, 103, 108, 115, 122, 128, 131, 132, 134, 140, 144, 149. Referred to throughout studies.

M

Mahayana Buddhism, 7.
Ma Kuei, 17.
Mathematics and Whitehead, 28, 31, 32, 47, 48, 129.
Ma Yüan, 14, 17, 19, 20.
Metamorphosis, 49, 54, 55, 56, 58, 68, 99, 126.
Metaphysics, XII, 24, 33, 45, 50, 51, 52, 72, 102, 108, 131, 146.
"Michael Angelo," 65. See Michelangelo, 95.
Mind (mental operations), 45, 49, 58, 75, 131, 133, 139, 142, 146.
Mind and matter, 49, 75, 76, 116, 139.
Monads, 49, 50, 74.
Monism, XIII, 25, 49, 51, 107.
Moritz, K. P., 47, 71, 91.
Morris, B., 145, 146.
Mutual immanence, 62, 70, 73, 119. See doctrine of internal relations.
Mysticism (mystic), XI, XIII, 1, 2, 3, 6, 10, 13, 19, 22, 25, 71, 103, 105, 107, 113, 120, 145, 149.

N

Necessity, 57, 86.
Negative prehensions, 28.